CW01083441

The Post War Touring Car

Previous page A Le Mans start traffic jam — the 1954 *Daily Express* meeting touring car race gets under way at Silverstone. Ken Wharton's Daimler Conquest Century ahead of Ian Appleyard's Jaguar Mk VII, and Lyndon Sims' 2½-litre Riley. But just look at the variety following up!

ISBN 0 85429 225 X

First published June 1977

©   Graham Robson 1977

The Haynes Publishing Group
Sparkford Yeovil Somerset BA22 7JJ England

distributed in the USA by
Haynes Publications Inc
9421 Winnetka Avenue
Chatsworth
California 91311 USA

a FOULIS Motoring Book

The majority of the text and photographs first appeared in issues of *Thoroughbred and Classic Cars* magazine. The IPC Transport Press have given us their kind permission to re-publish them here

Printed by J H Haynes and Company Limited Sparkford Yeovil Somerset BA22 7JJ
Bound by Cedric Chivers
Editor Tim Parker
Jacket design Phill Jennings

The Post War Touring Car

Graham Robson

Contents

Introduction

Please don't think this book is all about dull cars. That is not what I intend. Anyone leafing through these pages for an appreciation of VW Beetles, Morris Oxfords, Ford Consuls or almost any Vauxhall will be disappointed. This book looks deeper, at an altogether more significant breed of motoring.

My main aim is to try to break down the walls of prejudice. Do many of us have well-developed 'blind spots' when it comes to appreciating fine cars. Have we tended to ignore closed-car motoring for far too long? I have gradually become convinced that we have. We may all spend a lot of time enthusing over open-air motoring and the delights of splendid sports cars, but what do we actually drive?

Most of us, you can bet, drive around all day in closed cars! We may all look forward to a chance to swan around in the starkest of open cars, but from day to day we usually stay under cover. Is this hypocritical? I don't think so. The fact of the matter is that practicality usually comes first.

Most of us need the convenience of a wind-tight and weather-tight car, but that doesn't mean we have to be bored. To cater for people like me, and for millions of others all over the world, a particular breed of closed-in motoring has developed. To indulge in this, and whether the cars are advertised like that or not, we buy a Sports Saloon.

This is not merely a British quirk. In Italy, where you can rely on the weather for much of the year, open cars like the Fiat Spiders and 2-seat Alfa Romeos have virtually disappeared. In the country where appreciation of fine lines and a crisp exhaust note is so well developed, almost everyone hides under a tin top. In North America, even though there is an addiction to open-air anything (especially on the West Coast), legislation has virtually outlawed open cars. Cars specifically designed for North America - like the TR7 and the latest sporting Jaguars - hide their drivers from the elements. Sports car manufacturers like Alpine-Renault and Lancia all concentrate on coupes instead of sports cars.

INTRODUCTION

But where, when, and how did the new breed evolve? And what, indeed, should I call them? They could be 'sports saloons', they could be 'grand touring cars' or even 'GT' cars. But in delving into the lines of development, the successes and failures, the mainstream and the oddballs, I decided that I couldn't agree with any of these names. In the end they had to be 'Touring Cars' - and the reader will be able to add any nuances of his own.

I am afraid that this is rather a sad book. It could be that being so close to the modern product has made me rather cynical, but I don't discern the variety and interest in motoring nowadays that was definitely present in the 1950s. This book may not be an obituary, but it might be the final testament to a dying breed. I hope not.

I should acknowledge that the bare bones of this book have already been published - in part-work form by the magazine *Thoroughbred and Classic Cars*. I would like to thank IPC Transport Press Ltd., and the staff of *T & CC*, for their help, and for permission to reproduce the material and illustrations. My thanks to *Autocar* and *Motor* for original permission to plunder their extensive photographic libraries, and to *Autocar* in particular for the use of their splendid cutaway technical drawings. Finally, a tribute to Lionel Burrell, whose careful and artistic production of the part-work made the whole thing possible in the first place.

Graham Robson
Brampton
Cumbria
1977

Graham Robson.

Part 1
Setting the scene

*D*efining *the breed and looking back into history. How the sporting car became a touring car, and how the touring cars became interesting. The significance of the 1930s, and the most important models. Would post-war motoring be greatly different?*

I must begin with an unanswerable query - what exactly is a sports saloon? To coin a phrase made famous by Professor Joad of the BBC's *Brain Trust* - it all depends what you mean by 'sports'. So here I am, not even started in a development history, wondering about the scope of the subject!

A Bristol 405 is a sports saloon, but what about a Mark VII Jaguar? A Sunbeam Talbot 90 is a sports saloon, but what about a Triumph Vitesse? An MG Magnette looks safe, but what about a Riley Pathfinder? A Sunbeam Rapier? A 3-litre Lagonda? Does any Saab qualify? How about an Alfa 1900? You see, we have a problem.

It doesn't help that I have already decided to blur the edges of the survey. Perhaps a saloon doesn't really need to have four full-sized seats, and if there is a drop-head version we might include that as well. We can't possibly put a limitation on the mechanical layout, the size - or even whether the manufacturer originally intended to make a sports saloon or not. After all, 'Steady' Barker once came back from road testing a Daimler Limousine, I think it was, in 1963, and said it was the finest and fastest sports saloon he had yet driven. On the other hand there have been cars with 'GT' badges, or similar misnomers, plastered all over them, which were more impressive on Brighton Promenade than in a rally.

Everyone has had their stab at defining a sports car, and none of us do it well. I think it was Michael Sedgwick who suggested that any motoring writer's penance should be to write a short history of the motor car — perhaps he should then be asked to define sports motoring. *The Autocar* used to get into a terrible tangle on that subject — in 1956 Michael Brown once spent two whole pages adding all the variables, decided it was all up to the individual, and pointed out that a Ford Zephyr saloon must surely qualify because Gatsonides had won the Monte Carlo Rally in one!

Left Yes, perhaps it really was superior? George Brough's own idea of a high-class Grand Tourer, powered by a lazy American engine

A sheep in wolf's clothing, perhaps, but the 1½-litre MG saloons were very elegant machines. Underneath they were mainly Wolseley by 1939

A classic from first to last, Citroen's *traction avant* really set new handling standards

We must have a go at defining a sports saloon too, but not in any rigid manner. No doubt there will be dozens of letters either to contradict or to add more variations. In the *Autocar* earlier mentioned, Michael Brown listed these attributes:

High performance engine
Good power-weight ratio
Satisfying gear change
Smart appearance
Low centre of gravity
'Proper' instruments
Good brakes
Good cornering capabilities
A feeling of 'one-ness' with the driver
Complete safety.

    — he also went on to stress the importance of 'tradition', pointing out quite rightly   **13**

THE POST WAR TOURING CAR

A brave effort was Lea Francis' attempts to re-establish themselves after the Second War. Both these were for export

that some cars, like Alvis, kept a sporting reputation long after the product had changed significantly, while others like BMC and Rootes were having trouble establishing their own.

It begins to look as if others have already said enough for me. I would also add that a car is a sports saloon if its owner *thinks* it is one — and I don't find anything illogical in this remark. Surely we all treated our very first Minis like sports saloons in 1959 and 1960? And they were, surely? Nothing would personally convince me about Mark VII Jaguars — but Ronnie Adams won the Monte Carlo Rally in one, didn't he?

We also have to fudge the grey borderline between saloons and coupes. For the purposes of my argument I will call a coupe a saloon if I think it is one — and why not? Perhaps it can all be summarised from *'Through the Looking Glass' by Humpty Dumpty and Alice:*

"When *I* use a word," Humpty Dumpty said in rather a scornful tone, "it means just what I choose it to mean — neither more nor less."

"The question is," said Alice, "whether you *can* make words mean so many different things?"

After running Triumph for a short time, Donald Healey decided to strike out on his own. This was an early, and very successful design — the Healey Abbott

"The question is," said Humpty Dumpty, "which is to be Master — that's all."

Certainly, my definition includes a four-seat interior, or at least a two-plus-two layout which my children could find habitable. It doesn't matter whether the car should have two doors or four. But five? Fortunately, no-one built sporting estate cars until recently, and the Renault 16TS and Maxi HL are really saloons with a huge opening boot lid.

There is a lot of history involved. Up to the 1920s, of course, there were far fewer closed cars than tourers and convertibles, though as some cynics have pointed out they were all sports cars anyway; anyone ready to put up with repeated breakdowns and idiosyncracies had to be a sport! The saloon began to take over when ways were found of making the coachwork light enough so that rigidity was preserved along with performance. Once pressed-steel bodies had been developed, the saloon took over. From about 1928 to 1930, open-air motoring started a decline. The rot set in at low price levels first — where the cost penalty of making coachbuilt convertibles and tourers was already a discouragement.

15

Above Most of us could only afford Anglias,
Below when we might have liked Rover 10s and 12s

The first postwar Geneva Motor Show in 1947, but there are few new cars. Those are TA14 Alvises in foreground, with some of the worst excesses of 1940s Americana behind

Crème de la crème — a line up of Mk VI Bentleys and Rolls-Royce Silver Wraiths, at Crewe before a USA sales tour

THE POST WAR TOURING CAR

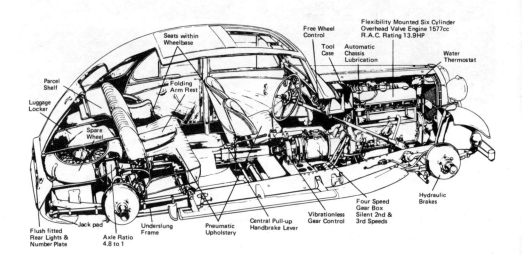

Seats within Wheelbase

Free Wheel Control

Flexibility Mounted Six Cylinder
Overhead Valve Engine 1577cc
R.A.C. Rating 13.9HP

Tool Case

Automatic Chassis Lubrication

Water Thermostat

Parcel Shelf

Folding Arm Rest

Luggage Locker

Spare Wheel

Hydraulic Brakes

Flush fitted Rear Lights & Number Plate

Jack pad

Axle Ratio 4.8 to 1

Underslung Frame

Pneumatic Upholstery

Central Pull-up Handbrake Lever

Vibrationless Gear Control

Four Speed Gear Box Silent 2nd & 3rd Speeds

Not fashionable, but with all the right ideas, was Rover's Speed 14 Streamline Coupe of 1934

Motoring legend, sketchily supported, has it that all motoring in the 1930s was dull, but careful observation proves otherwise. As far as we are concerned, indeed, the sports saloon really became established at all levels. The first sports saloons were built on big expensive chassis, where a bit of excess weight was no matter — we remember the big 6½-litre Bentleys, Sunbeams, Hispano-Suizas, and even a few Rolls-Royces as splendid examples. However, by the 1930s, the right sort of motoring, under cover, started to evolve in Coventry (SS, Riley, Triumph and the like), at Abingdon (MG), in Thames Ditton and Staines (AC and Lagonda), West London (Talbot) and all over Europe. All seemed to agree that looks were important, along with a bright and interesting performance and good handling. At the time, too, one could almost write into the definition that interior space should be a mite cramped, as styling and aerodynamics sometimes took precedence over the people who had to pay the bills!

There are those who would aver that the best-ever sports saloon motoring could be had at H.M. Government's expense in the 1940s — quite a few well-known and well-respected figures found new pleasures in things as diverse as a Daimler Scout car, or a

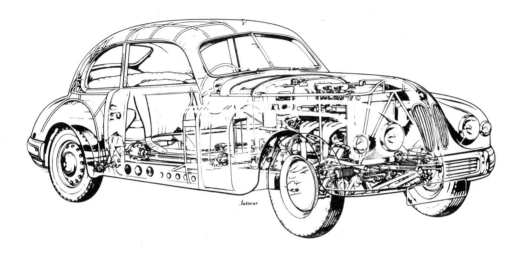

By aeronautics out of BMW — Bristol's famous 401/403 series. This is the 403

Churchill tank; even a Jeep or a big staff car had its charms.

Even those of us too young really to understand why, decided we didn't like the way North American styling developed in the 1940s and 1950s, so it is hardly surprising that the classic sports saloons from this side of the Atlantic had smooth lines and understated details. Not that we could actually drive them at once, but only admire from afar. The 1940s, in particular, were when we had to Export or Die (politicians were no more inventive than they are now) — and among the exports were Bristol 400s and 401s. Allards, Riley 1½s and 2½s, Sunbeams, Jaguars, Bentleys, Jensens, even Armstrong Siddeleys and Daimlers. Lagondas, Alvises and Aston-Martings were built in tiny numbers.

The Big Six, as it then was, found out about this sort of car in the 1950s, and set about debasing the currency with the first Sunbeam Rapiers and the Standard Vanguard Sportsman, but it was not until the end of the decade that things took a turn for the better. The North American planning influence finally infiltrated, the concept of making a multitude of models from one basic design was accepted, and more or less by chance a whole new series of race- and rally-winning sports saloons evolved. Mini-Coopers and

19

The Jowett Javelin was an immediate post war flash of brilliance. It didn't sell more than 30,000 examples but it had a good competition record including class wins in the 1949 and 1951 Monte Carlo Rallies

The Aston Martin DB2 series — race proved at Le Mans before they went into production. One of our all-time favourites, first seen in 1950. That is a DB Mk3 Convertible behind, and the circuit is Silverstone

Lotus-Cortinas already have their own reputation in Valhalla, along with lesser successes like Vauxhall VX4/90s, Triumph 2.5PIs, Riley 1.5s and the like. To them you have to add Jaguar 3.4s and 3.8s, with cars from Mercedes-Benz, Lancia, Fiat and the small specialists.

For the moment, I want to run through the cars which evolved in the 1930s, and which even the VSCC admit as 'thoroughbreds'. In Britain, the palm must go to Sir William Lyons for the way he built up a complete new *marque* (SS) at a time when many old manufacturers were struggling for survival. SS started as nothing better than rakishly re-bodied Standards, but by 1939 had become complete cars in their own right. Sir William realised from the start that looks were everything in the 1930s, and his SS-Jaguars were copied by others before 1939. Riley had more tradition than most in the 1930s, and produced some startlingly beautiful styles hiding excellently-efficient engines, before financial trouble forced them into Lord Nuffield's empire. Triumph, their neighbours in Coventry, built a series of elegant Glorias, Vitesses and Dolomites, before they too went

21

THE POST WAR TOURING CAR

The Aston Martin Atom, designed in 1939 and 1940, was killed by the David Brown takeover

bankrupt, though ironically it was MG's move to sports saloons which made sure they survived in 1935 and onwards!

The British sports saloon might have been no quicker than cars from Europe, but most of us would agree that they were better styled. It is always a matter of opinion, of course, but the type of elegant body produced for Alvis, Bentley, Jensen, Lagonda, and Talbot was often the envy of the world. There was a tradition (that word again) in British coachbuilding which had been breeding elegant stylists for generations. The Second World War acted as a watershed to the coachbuilding industry, because of the social changes it heralded, and from 1945 the British lead was lost. At the same time the economics of individuality-built cars went mad, and the exclusive body, like the couturier-made gown, began to disappear. The really striking sports saloon is now seen at a Motor Show, and rarely thereafter.

There were straws in the wind in the 1930s. We saw the first examples of Anglo-American design thinking where cheap powerful North American engineering was

An Austin 16, this was actually announced in August 1939 with a 12hp engine

preferred to exquisite hand-built British units. Railton and Jensen were pioneers - there is therefore nothing startling nor advanced about a Gordon-Keeble, a Jensen CV-8 or an Iso Rivolta. There was also the poignant lesson that elegance and mechanical excellence rarely attracts profits; what happened to Lagonda in 1947 and Facel Vega in the 1960s had already happened to Bentley and Sunbeam in the 1930s. There was also evidence that a quantity-produced car like a Sunbeam-Talbot could be as nicely styled and as popular as the tiny-production device which owed existence to a coachbuilder and a benevolent banker!

When peace broke out in 1945, the market had changed radically. Apart from the much higher cost of materials and labour compared with 1939, there was a drastic shortage, seemingly, of *everything*. Purchase tax was levelled savagely against anything like a sports saloon that could be described as 'luxury goods', and social revolution was at hand. Would motoring for pleasure survive?

23

Guaranteed to make die-hard MG enthusiasts shudder in 1953, but what a fine car the Magnette was

The splendid coupe derivative of a not-very-pretty saloon — Lancia's Monte Carlo Rally winning Aurelia GT 2.5-litre

Quite startlingly beautiful when seen in 1960, the Bertone-bodied Gordon was the first European-American

Ian Fleming loved his, and if you have enough money they are still available in the States, Studebaker's Avanti

Certainly Grand for Touring, so does that make this Daimler a GT?

This was MG's Y-Type saloon of the late 1940s, based closely on Morris Eight and Ten bits, but with the XPAG engine. The TD sports car evolved from a shortened version of this chassis ...

Part 2
Survivors and young hopefuls - the 1940s

In 1945 the motor industry started again. Tools of old models came out of store, and a few new models were announced. But times were hard. Would sporting motoring ever be the same again?

The Hitler war changed everything. I make no excuse for opening with a remark like that. What happened from 1939 to 1945, what caused the fighting, and what was needed to win the battle, affected everything that has happened since. Certainly the sort of motoring we enjoyed in 1939, and the privation we accepted in the 1940s, were very different. Changes in the motoring climate were startling and sudden. It was as if an all-powerful dictator had decreed that pleasure should be abolished, that no one with money to spare should be allowed to enjoy it; and that sporting cars should be doled out like cigarettes at an inquisition.

No car firm went broke because of the war, but several didn't survive the peace. It was all so dull, and it was all to do with a drastic steel shortage. We had to Export or Die (even the speeches were made in capital letters!) - and steel allocations were according to that dictum. It was quite obvious that small-production, low-export car firms were in trouble.

The hopefuls without cash nor strategy disappeared at once. There might have been a few Altas, Brough Superiors, Atalantas and Raymond Mays in 1939, but they were never seen again. The technological marvels like vee-12 Lagondas and Phantom III Rolls-Royces went on to a motoring Valhalla, and even the special delights of a Derby Bentley were submerged in a productivity drive at Crewe.

Supply difficulties in 1945 and 1946 were quite horrific, but it didn't stop a few young hopefuls starting up. The secret was aluminium bodywork (it was principally a *sheet* steel shortage - steel or iron for castings, forgings and tubes was easier to find), the

The MG's facia betraying all the signs of 1930s coachcraft thinking. But at least the steering column was adjustable for length ...

The 1948 line-up of Lea Francis cars. Hugh Rose designed the engine, and Lea Francis did their own styling. Fine cars, but too expensive

Sydney Allard's productionised 'Specials' sold well in the 1940s. This was a K2 with Cadilac engine, actually built in 1951

THE POST WAR TOURING CAR

Understated, and almost pre-war styling, W. O. Bentley's Lagonda had a timeless elegance. Happily, David Brown kept this design for years after he took over the company

right sort of car for export, and a lot of optimism. Some of the new cars appeared so quickly that there were only two explanations - either they had been developed before the war, or during the 'midnight oil' period, or they had been designed in time stolen from military work towards the end of the fighting when the pressures were lifting!

Within a year, Britain had three new manufacturers Allard, Bristol, and Healey - not only with new prototypes but with cars delivered to prove their point. They evolved in different ways - Allard by productionising his 1939 'Special', Bristol by leaning heavily on imported BMW engineering, and Healey by a resourceful 'scissors and paste' job from other firms' parts. Healey, for one, made no secret of the time spent in design - original layouts were on Hillman-Humber drawing boards during the war years!

Lagonda abandoned their exotic 4½-litre vee-12 with reluctance, but had high hopes of a new car built around W.O. Bentley's fine new twin-cam 2½-litre 'six'. Nearby, Invicta rose like a phoenix from the ashes of Railton (and don't forget that Railton started where Invicta finished in the early 1930s!) - their Black Prince prototype was exciting, even if few trusted the weird Brockhouse transmission, nor Invicta's ability to produce the splendid twin-cam 3-litre engine.

Jaguar soon got going again with their stylish saloons, but dropped the SS100 sports car, and Rootes kept on with the 1939-style Sunbeam-Talbots (though the bigger models slipped into Humber and limbo). Sir John Black bought the bombed-out remains

Styled around the package of a pre-war Standard Flying Twelve, the Triumph 1800 was the only mass-produced attempt at razor-edge styling in the 1940s. The car later inherited the Vanguard engine

of Triumph in 1945, producing the first Standard-Triumphs (the 1800s) in 1946. The really nice surprise from Coventry was a pair of sleek new Rileys - which used the splended 1½-litre and 2½-litre 'fours' developed during the 1930s. The surprise was nice because 1939 Rileys had been rather horrid: Lord Nuffield had bought the company when its money ran out in 1938, and the hastily revamped cars were Wolseleys with a new nose and Riley engines. But here was something quite different.

Completing Coventry's scene were the low-production Lea-Francis cars with their Riley-like engines, and some remarkably interesting Armstrong-Siddeleys that could easily have been thought sporting if they hadn't come from such a stodgy stable! At the other side of the city, Alvis looked around their crowded Holyhead Road premises, realised that they were now making more money from aero-engines than from cars, and decided to make even fewer than they had previously. Everyone was sorry to see the last of those magnificent 3½-litre and 4.3-litre six-cylinder cars, but at least the new 'Fourteen' was very like the pre-war 12-70 series. Alvis hadn't lost interest in six-cylinder sports saloons, but their new car did not appear until 1950.

In the hard times of 1945 and 1946 this was very encouraging, even if the waiting lists and 'covenant schemes' were depressing. But in 1947 enthusiasts were astonished by an entirely new car from Jowett - something quite unconnected with their down-to-earth 1930s products. The new Javelin was conceived by Gerald Palmer (himself an ex-MG

THE POST WAR TOURING CAR

Jensen styling had its moments — the 1949 Interceptor was hardly one of them! Under the bonnet was an Austin 4-litre engine. The Austin A40 sports came from the same drawing board

designer) in 1942 and 1943. It was Jowett's only post-war car, but it leaned far more to a sporting concept than could have been hoped. It had smooth modern styling, a flat-four engine not merely because Jowett engines always were flat but because it was an efficient space-saver, and it had torsion bar ifs which worked very well.

By 1947 Britain was deep in economic gloom, with heavy overseas debts, food shortages and a coal supply crisis (so what's new about the present situation?), and we still had to export everything we could possibly sell. Car designers were not encouraged to be clever when it was clear that world markets were willing to buy almost any car they could find. On the other hand, imports of anything except food and essentials was discouraged, and the car market saw nothing of the famous European Grand Tourers which had been so *chic* in the 1930s. Not that they would have been encouraged from Italy or Germany for obvious reasons though the RAF had flattened their factories anyway and the famous old cars couldn't be made. *The Autocar* Buyers' Guide in October 1948 only listed seven imported European *marques* of which only Renault was serious.

Before 1948, there was little technical advance to salute. Most cars built were pre-war designs, or new cocktails of old ideas. But Earls Court was scheduled for the autumn - the first Motor Show for ten years - and something was expected to make headlines. That 'something' as it happened, was the advanced little Morris Minor (which

Invicta's exciting Black Prince, with startling engineering and technical bravery, did not survive the 1940s

It had a very advanced engine, with twin-overhead camshafts, and triple SU carbs. Note! Twin plugs and twin distributors on this engine

THE POST WAR TOURING CAR

At the end of the 1940s Lancia were preoccupied with the smooth Aurelia; its coupe derivative, the exciting GT, followed a couple of years later

Lord Nuffield never liked), and William Lyons' beautifully effective XK120 sports car. The Issigonis-designed Minor offered new standards of handling and response which made almost every other touring car feel like a pensioned-off heap, and the Jaguar engine was quite obviously designed for great exploits in the future.

At the same time, there were disappointments. Neither Aston Martin nor Lagonda had survived, but David Brown was now wedding the best of each design together, behind closed doors, for his new DB2, which would be seen at Le Mans in 1949. Invicta folded after a few of their Black Prince cars had been made, while Jensen's Meadows-engined PW model was definitely a Myth instead of a Hit. Healeys were nice but rare. Jowetts were nice, but fragile, and there wasn't a sporting Bentley in sight. The sleek P3 Rover was to become the podgy P4 soon afterwards, so it was left to Sunbeam-Talbot to restore a bit of hope, even if their new '80' and '90' didn't get independent front suspension until 1950. Singer, Standard and Wolseley had nothing to say, though Nuffield's little MG YA saloon was nice. The least said about *any* other Austin, Ford, Morris or Vauxhall the better.

Before Britain had to face the competition of European imports, its sporting saloons had to improve, and we must be glad they did. For the 1950s, independent front suspension was necessary, as were high-output engines, light structures, and styling whose

By Bristol out of BMW — the first Bristol 400 design. Here driven by the Duke of Richmond and Gordon when opening the Goodwood track in 1948

lines had been drawn after the war when outlooks and optimisms had returned to normal. True, we had to endure petrol rationing until May 1950, ludicrous waiting for a new car (five to seven years for the most desirable), and shortages of just about everything, but with the Monte Carlo Rally revived in 1949, and an RAC Rally promised for 1951, things were surely looking up?

Allard expanded, winning races and rallies, Alvis finally produced their elegant 3-litre more touring than sporting, but new throughout, and Aston Martin got their splendid DB2 coupe into production. Bristol progressed logically from the Type 400 to the 401, Sunbeam-Talbot improved the '90' with ifs and a bigger engine, while Jowett's Javelin was joined by the ERA-designed Jupiter. Jensen, meantime, had introduced their Interceptor, with a big Austin 4-litre engine; it might not have been too exclusive but it was at least reliable and available.

But in 1950 the big news came from Jaguar. Two years earlier they had produced the XK120, but at the same time a new and very smart Mark V saloon with the old push-rod engines. Here, at last, was the new saloon car for which the XK engine had always been intended - the big and strikingly-styled Mark VII. To look at its bulk and its weight, this was a car which had no right to be sporting, but with its magnificent Heynes—Hassan—designed engine, and a comfortable 100 mph-plus maximum speed (all

THE POST WAR TOURING CAR

The Triumph that wasn't! Donald Healey designed his own car during the war, and hoped Triumph would build it. They didn't. Healey built it himself, with Riley 2½-litre mechanicals and a 100 mph performance. This is the Westland convertible

for an astonishingly modest selling price) how could one deny its merits?

So here were the sporting tourers for the 1950s. Looking back from the wisdom of another twenty years, it is easy to suggest that they were not a very inspiring lot, but it is always necessary to look at the run-of-the-mill cars for comparison. Was there really *anything* worth buying from Longbridge ... or Dagenham ... or Cowley ... or Luton ... or Canley? A look down the entry for that first post-war RAC Rally (run off in June 1951) shows up many Jaguars, Sunbeam-Talbots, Healeys, MGs, Jowetts, Allards and Rileys - probably as many as the potential entrants could get their hands on in time for the event - and logically enough there were very few imported cars. Incidentally, there were no fewer than 52 Jaguars (of 266 entries) - a measure of the way the XK engine, in sports car or saloon, had come to dominate the sporting scene.

For the time being, then, the problem was not so much selling the cars but actually building and delivering them. Prices were high enough compared with the 1930s (a 3½-litre Jaguar saloon cost £445 in 1938, and £988 ten years later before tax) but since then the hated purchase tax had arrived. Its rate fluctuated over the years, but in 1950 any car suffered a 33 per cent imposition on its ex-factory price; worse was to come.

The industry, in the main, was technically behind the times. As yet there was little evidence of advanced design in engines in suspensions or in structures. The age-old layout reigned supreme - engine at front, drive at rear live axle with half-eliptic springs, and a solid pressed-steel separate chassis. But there were twinkles in many a designer's eye. Time, opportunity, prosperity and a bit of optimism would work wonders. Big changes were brewing for the 1950s.

What is it? It's a Marauder sports car — one of only fifteen. Built in Warwickshire and based on a Rover 75 chassis and mechanicals, the Marauder was Peter Wilks' and George Mackie's dream car. Peter Wilks at the wheel in this 1950 picture, George Mackie on his right and Richard Mead on his left

Two Dutch and one British Jowett Javelin finishing a Tulip Rally in the car park of the hotel Huis ter Duin at Noordwyk

3-litre Alvis and Jaguar Mk VII tackling the Hunze Rug in the reverse direction on the Zandvoort Circuit — Tulip Rally 1954

Part 3
Race and rally successes -
1950 to 1955

***P**rosperity returns, the new models arrive, and sales increase dramatically. An end to gloom and a return to motoring for enjoyment. New cheap sporting tourers from all quarters. Competition for publicity, and to improve the breed. Vintage years for the British touring car.*

It is all very well boasting about a country's exciting touring cars, but sooner or later you have to prove it. The British had a difficult time in the late 1940s. There were few races or rallies as yet - and how do you set about convincing a buyer when Tulip Rally regulations allow ancient-style Ford Anglias to win?

In the 1950s, the climate for motoring improved rapidly. Gloom changed to optimism, petrol came off the ration, waiting lists shortened, and new-car choice widened. Behind-the-scenes research began to bear fruit, and the second generation of post-war designs started to filter through. Happily, there were few mergers to kill off the esoteric cars. It wasn't yet the time of "never had it so good", but all the portents pointed that way.

From 1951 to 1955, the cars we bought became more and more interesting. There was still little sign of interest in 'sports saloon' motoring from the Big Six, with the exception of Nuffield and Sunbeam-Talbot, but the variety from a still-sizeable independent industry was gratifying and satisfying. There were lots of new models, some developments of those already shown by 1950, but some startling surprises.

I suppose it was logical that Bentley should stray off the staid and narrow with their first delectable Continental coupes, that Lagonda should restyle their all-independent saloon and give it a 3-litre engine. Bristol were expected to evolve faster versions of the 401 - named the 403 - and it was only a matter of time before BMC's rationalisation should strike MG and Riley. It was also to be expected that Alfa Romeo, Lancia and Mercedes-Benz would spring back to prominence, though we were all disappointed that BMW showed no signs of their illustrious past.

All this was fine, and predictable, but the British enthusiast was in for a number of very pleasant surprises. Time for a detailed look shortly, but how many of us could have

A Grand way to go Touring? One of several fine, but expensive cars from Daimler in the 1950s. This one was a special bodied Regency, styling by Hooper

Lady Docker's 1952 Show car — a Hooper-bodied coupe Daimler straight eight

A special bodied Lancia by Touring (like the ZA Magnette?)

Lancia Aurelia GT — lengthened by Pinin Farina

Above Jensen's 541, first of a whole family and
Below its fairly spartan interior

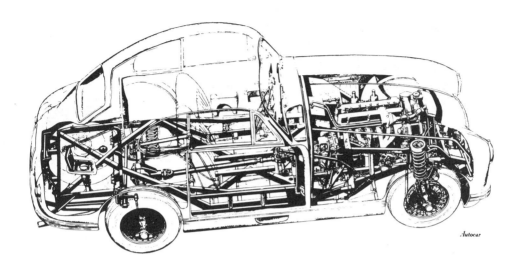

The Aston Martin DB2 laid bare — W. O. Bentley's Lagonda twin-ohc engine, allied to Claude Hill's multi-tube chassis

hoped for a new 100 mph saloon from Alvis, a technically interesting sports saloon from Armstrong-Siddeley (and even more way-out models promised for 1956), an ultra-modern close-coupled four-seater coupe from Jensen that *really* went, a mouth-watering "businessman's express" from Bristol, or - most surprising of all - a sports saloon *and* a competition programme from Daimler?

In the world of competition motoring, we soon became used to Jaguar, Aston-Martin and Bristol exploits with their specialised racing two seaters, and in production car racing it was soon a case of Mark VII Jaguars winning everything, with another motor race going on astern. In the rallying business, where endurance, strength and adaptability counted for much, our cars soon began to chalk up success. Ian Appleyard became Europe's best-known rally driver - winning seemingly innumerable events with the same XK120; this famous old car, NUB 120 (which now lives in retirement in the National Motor Museum), completed three seasons with the same chassis, the same body and the same venerable old engine - they don't make RS1800s like that any more! Sports cars won most of the rallies because they were quick and strong, but in the Monte Carlo Rally driving skill often made up for the difference.

Sydney Allard drove himself into the record books in 1952, with one virtuoso performance in a heavy old P1 Allard saloon, to win the Monte. Allard had performed valiantly in races and trials even before the Hilter war, and won the RAC Hillclimb championship in 1949, but this one win did more for him than any other. It broke all sorts of records too - the first time the Monte had been won by anyone in his own make of car, and the first time by a British car since Donald Healey in a "flat-iron" Invicta in 1931. Allard beat Stirling Moss' works Sunbeam-Talbot 90 entry by just four seconds on

45

THE POST WAR TOURING CAR

An almost mythical beast — the fabulous but rare Spanish Pegaso. We never saw them in Britain

the last, two-hour regularity test, where cars without studs or chains had to tackle ice and snow at average speeds approaching 30 mph non-stop. And it wasn't an "easy year" either - only fifteen cars actually arrived in Monte Carlo without loss of time on the road section.

That year it wasn't only Allard and Moss, for Jaguar Mark VII (Cotton) finished fourth, Jowett Jupiter (Becquart) was fifth, and another Mark VII was sixth.

A year later, Britain did it again, this time with Dutchman Maurice Gatsonides driving a works Ford Zephyr. The gap was even tighter than ever - a mere one second over Ian Appleyard's Mark VII Jaguar - and Vard's Mark VII was fifth and Moss' Sunbeam-Talbot sixth. 1953 was an easy year - there was little snow even in the Alps behind Monte Carlo, and Gatso's Zephyr needed bucket-water-cooling of its drum brakes at several points on the mountain circuit!

The year after that Chiron's Lancia Aurelia coupe won the event - after an enormous row which centred around whether or not the car was truly in production in that form - but in 1955 it was Rootes' turn when a privately-entered Sunbeam Mk 3 (the last of the S-T 90 variants - remember?) took the premier award.

The rallying and the racing fraternity were soon to get used to the idea of factory support for a team of saloons - some, like the Zephyrs and Austin A50s, the most unlikely machinery at first glance - but it took a lot of getting accustomed to the presence of Alvis, Armstrong-Siddeley and Daimler as well. Armstrong's flirtation with factory support was yet to come (and Tommy Sopwith had much to do with this), but in 1953 - 1955 the Alvis Grey Lady and the Daimler Conquest Century came to prominence.

Neither looked very sporting at first, though the Alvis at least was always a very

The BMW 501

sleek saloon in the classic traditions. In spite of their high prices and their select clientele (a Grey Lady cost £1,822, and a Conquest Century £1,661 in good 1950s currency), both cars handled well enough, and proved agreeably tuneable, for them to be campaigned seriously. It was Dunham and Banks who performed well in the Alvises, but Daimler even sponsored a works team in 1954, which included such stalwarts as Reg Parnell, George Abecassis, Ken Wharton, and Nancy Mitchell. The Conquest Century (Conquest because it originally cost £1,066 basic, and Century because of the power output, 100bhp!) won its class in the 1954 *Daily Express* Production Car Race, beating off some 2½-litre Rileys in the process. The car's chassis was completely conventional - no disc brakes yet, of course, though a rather novel form of laminated torsion bar front suspension undoubtedly helped, and the gearbox was the generation-old Daimler fluid flywheel and pre-selector layout. The engine, though, was an all-new in-line six-cylinder of 2433 cc with conventional ohv operation and twin SU carburettors. But Daimler management was in very weird hands in those days (remember the Docker Daimlers, and the boardroom revolution that soon followed?) - the Century was a fine car which was undersold, while on the other hand the Conquest Roadster, which evolved from it, was never properly developed. Daimler lost their opportunity to break further into *our* sort of market, and the cars grew inexorably larger and less nimble.

The same, fortunately, could not be said of the Bristols. The original Type 400 had really been an updated BMW, though the 401, 402 Convertible, and 403 were fine cars engineered at Bristol. So far so good, and very nice too, but towards the end of 1953 Bristol startled the motoring world with their sleek and dramatically fast 404 Coupe. Everyone raved about it at the time, though it could only command limited sales due to a

47

The new and the old, Bristol's 403 and 404 in 1953

A good new breed? The MG ZA Magnette, Wolseley-based but a sports-saloon none the less

The classic nose of an Alfa Romeo 1900 (Coupe body by Farina)

THE POST WAR TOURING CAR

Elegance in the grand manner — the 1952 Bentley Continental

strict two-seater layout and a first cost, in 1953, of £2,350 (basic). (For comparison, a Jaguar XK120 coupe cost a mere £1,140. The Bristol-built frame was immensely rigid, the handling of a high standard, and the looks beyond reproach. Pundits loved the tiny tail fins, and suggested that the fashion might spread (it did, but not for functional reasons). Performance, with the optional 125bhp engine - and this, from only 1971cc - was quite outstanding. With maximum speed of around 120 mph. Yet very few were sold, as the later version of this car, the long-wheelbase four-door 405 saloon, was that much more practical and even cost around £150 less! We don't have 405s any more, of course, but the few 411s still made have much detail engineering which dates back to the 404 and 1953. *The Autocar* called the 404 a "Collector's piece" in 1954, while it was still in small-scale production - we must surely agree with them now. Incidentally, this was one of the first cars we knew which had Michelin X radial-ply tyres as standard equipment..

Getting back to more normal selling prices, and the sort of motoring many of us could afford, it was sad to see BMC's dead hand descend on Abingdon. The 2½-litre Riley gave way to the Wolseley-based Pathfinder ("ditchfinder" was the pet name, and we won't argue with that), and the sweet if innocuous MG YB saloon, really a 1930s design, finally disappeared. But wasn't it a nice surprise to see the YB replaced by a fine new sporting saloon, the ZA Magnette? The purists, of course, objected to the use of a classic old name, and said the car wasn't really an MG anyway but a Wolseley (what about the WA, VA and SA in the 1930s then?); it didn't have an MG engine, but an Austin engine, and anyway it didn't *look* like an MG did it?

All of which might have made sense if the MG Magnette hadn't been a spritely, sure-footed and above all fairly swift machine. By the time Marcus Chambers' Abingdon

The smart and spritely Armstrong-Siddeley Star Sapphire

Competitions Department had learned how to tune 'B' Type engines, and to keep the brakes in one piece, the Magnette was a sports saloon of which to be proud.

Truly, our standards were looking up, but this was none too soon. Imports were beginning to arrive in some numbers, among them the latest in Alfa Romeo (the 1900 and the jewel-like little Giulietta), Lancia (the 2½-litre Aurelia GT), Fiat (a few 1100TVs and even an occasional 8V Coupe), plus of course, the sensational Mercedes-Benz 300SL. The gull-winged Merc. wasn't quite as mythical as the Spanish Pegasos, which never reached us, but its performance was subject to as much exaggeration. I remember reading that the Le Mans 300SL prototypes had been capable of more than 160 mph, then reading in 1954 that production cars with fuel injection could reach 165 mph. Next I read *The Autocar* Road Test (of 25 March, 1955), saw a mean maximum speed of 'only' 129 mph, and felt very cheated! It would be another ten years before any production coupe could get up to 150 mph without special tuning and preparation. The 300SL didn't handle very well either, with its simple swinging axle irs, but was so quick in a straight line that most of its owners didn't need to press their bravery around corners.

But if it did nothing else, the 300SL pointed the way ahead. Conventional engineering really wasn't going to be good enough later in the 1950s. Jaguar already had disc brakes on their racing machines (as did Triumph on Le Mans TR2s) Lucas were pushing fuel injection throughout the industry, and some way would soon have to found of improving roadholding and of shedding a lot of excess weight. The economic times were becoming increasingly hard, too, and it looked as if the cars would have to give better value in future. The TR2 and Austin-Healey sports cars had shown how it could be done - would the better touring cars soon follow suit?

Jaguar's brilliant XK engine, in 3 x SU 3.8-litre display form. Need we say more?

Part 4
Technical innovation
in the 1950s

*U*p to 1955 the best Touring cars used pre-war design techniques. From 1955 modern designs matured. The new generation of models was exciting.

In our own motor industry, the design revolution came in the 1950s. Left to themselves, no doubt, British tycoons would have carried on selling their out-of-date but easy-to-build cars. Changing this attitude took time, but in the end it was public pressure, and competition from the latest European imports, which persuaded them to change. Perhaps even the motoring press can take some credit. There was no instant change of heart, but I would say that the climate for innovation improved dramatically in 1954 and 1955. But for a time, with car sales suffering a mild recession, and even a spot of petrol rationing, the design and development teams beavered away behind the scenes.

Up to then, you could usually recognise pre-war design thinking in any popular sports-touring car. In many new models introduced from 1956 onwards, this wasn't possible. Designers had always been keen to advance - now, for the first time, it seemed, management actually approved, and the customer demand was healthy. There was another factor - every car designer depends to a great extent on the supply of specialised parts, and there seemed to be important developments brewing at all sides. Dunlop and Girling were ready with disc brakes, and Michelin with radial-ply tyres. Glass-fibre coachwork made small-production runs economic, and styling changes cheap. The 'Big Six' could now supply their own engines and other mechanical items to little firms quite unable to make their own. It was all very exciting. Would this be a new Golden Age like the 1920s? A new Vintage, perhaps?

A few of the modern technical miracles didn't catch on. The pundits, and many of the unthinking motoring press, greeted Mercedes-Benz' complicated space-frame chassis as an enormous advance. On the 300SL it worked well because the car was a closed car, but

53

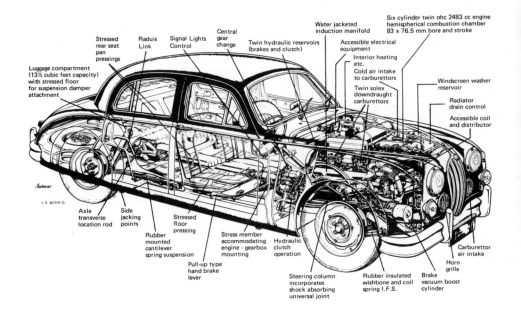

Luggage compartment
(13½ cubic feet capacity)
with stressed floor
for suspension damper
attachment

Stressed
rear seat
pan
pressings

Raduis
Link

Signal Lights
Control

Central
gear
change

Twin hydraulic reservoirs
(brakes and clutch)

Water jacketed
induction manifold

Six cylinder twin ohc 2483 cc engine
hemispherical combustion chamber
83 x 76.5 mm bore and stroke

Accessible electrical
equipment

Interior heating
etc.

Cold air intake
to carburettors

Twin solex
downdraught
carburettors

Windscreen washer
reservoir

Radiator
drain control

Accessible coil
and distributor

Autocar

V.R. BERRIS

Axle
transverse
location rod

Side
jacking
points

Stressed
floor
pressing

Rubber
mounted
cantilever
spring suspension

Stress member
accommodating
engine - gearbox
mounting

Hydraulic
clutch
operation

Pull-up type
hand brake
lever

Steering column
incorporates
shock absorbing
universal joint

Rubber insulated
wishbone and coil
spring I.F.S.

Brake
vacuum boost
cylinder

Carburettor
air intake

Horn
grille

Sir William's first monocoque Jaguar — the 1955 2.4

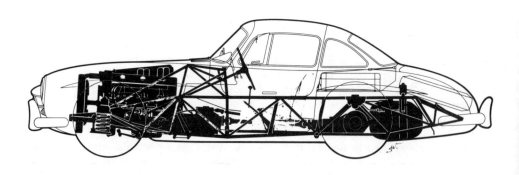

Mercedes-Benz' startlingly advanced 300SL, raced in 1954. No other company adopted the complex
space-frame chassis construction

Girling disc brakes on the Austin Healey 3000 in 1959 — a great advance in safety and performance

it was less successful when an open version was proposed. Anyway, even Mercedes-Benz didn't pursue that line of development any further. It was originated in their racing department for the 300SL sports prototypes, and somehow slipped through to be made in reasonable quantities on the production lines. The W196 Grand Prix car followed suit, as did the 300SLR sports-racer, but that was all. No other company adopted the pure space-frame construction method for a production car though such chassis were very popular among the racing car builders until the early 1960s. Cars like Aston Martin DB2 series, the AC Greyhound 2 + 2 Coupe, and Gilberns, used multi-tube frames, but these made no pretence to scientific stressing or layout. Cars like Jaguar's C Type, and the Peerless GTs were built in very small quantities using similar methods.

In the main, the design of chassis layouts stagnated. New models like XK140s and XK150s relied on existing 'Forth Bridge' structures, while Jensen and AC stuck strictly to traditional fabricated tubular systems. Triumph, for their TR1, actually used up redundant 1930s Standard Nine frames on their first prototype.

Colin Chapman (who else?) was the greatest innovator of the decade, and startled us all with his new Elite in 1957. Its monocoque hull would not have been so mind-

55

THE POST WAR TOURING CAR

The AC Greyhound — an elegant 2+2 Coupe announced for the 1960s

bending if it had not been built from reinforced glassfibre! It was altogether of Colin Chapman in the 1950s that technical innovation came before practicality - the Elite's hull was very strong, but proved difficult and expensive to make, and suffered badly from the refinement problems still plaguing the industry. Incidentally, Chapman was not the first to specify glassfibre bodywork for a production car - this distinction went to Jensen with their 541 in 1954 in the UK even if the first 541 prototype was panelled in light alloy and Chevrolet in the US for the 1953 Corvette.

A monocoque in glassfibre might be very rare, but the concept of a unit construction shell made up of many steel pressings welded together was catching on fast. Tiny independent constructors were not in any rush to adopt this principle themselves, as structures made in this way demanded huge tooling investment. Cars designed in this way tended to be built in large numbers; once a basic style was settled, regular styling changes were discouraged on the grounds of excess cost. This was really the beginning of the era, still continuing, where cars were given longer and uninterrupted runs.

Therefore, there was no way that Alvis, Bristol or Armstrong Siddeley would make such a revolutionary change. On the other hand, MG, Jaguar, Riley and Porsche were already committed, and behind the scenes there were similar projects in Austin-Healey,

The Greyhound's interior — wooden wheels were very chic at the time

Rootes and others. In the end, this complicated decision hinged on weight, strength, ease of manufacture - and a gamble on the length of production run that might be assumed. Finance apart, there was no doubt that unit construction shells were much more rigid than any other variety - compare, for instance, a Sprite with an old MG TF, an MGB with an MGA, a 1959 'Rootes' Alpine with the earlier Sunbeam-Talbot type.

The story in connection with engines was less encouraging. In the first ten years after the war, inventors fell over themselves to propose new units - with the gas turbine looking the most promising. In Britain, only Rover were seriously involved, and their first effort - JET1, the much modified Rover 75 - was no sports car. True, when boosted to a high output, the car achieved 150 mph on the Jabbeke high-way, but its economy (or lack of it) was a problem. A few years later, in 1956, Spen King designed T3, that one-off coupe which has happily survived to this day. T3, as it was coded, was everything a sports-saloon buyer might have wanted if only he could buy a replica - the car had nice styling, four-wheel drive, four-wheel disc brakes, and an exciting specification. It was also demonstrably a car of the 'fifties, without a single component looking back to good old tradition. But alas for Rover, their technical bravery was never rewarded - the engines were always horrifyingly expensive to build and only marginally economical enough on fuel

A drophead Citroen DS — sensationally sleek at the time

The rather special interior of British-built DS cars, 1961

The start of a real motor race! Actually the Zandvoort test on the 1959 Tulip Rally, with eventual winner Donald Morely (3.4 Jaguar, DJM 400) on the left of the grid

at first.

But the most useful of all the new components was the disc brake. Braking, particularly from high speeds and with drums hidden inside steel disc wheels, was a huge problem. Not even the most sophisticated materials would perform well indefinitely - a completely new technique was needed. But there was nothing new about discs. The Lanchester brothers had propounded their principle around the turn of the century, and even with the most sophisticated heat exchangers installed.

Rotary motion was the ideal - one where the reciprocating action of pistons and connecting rods could be abolished completely - but no one achieved this. Even the Wankel engine, revealed right at the end of the 1950s by Felix Wankel, is not truly rotary - and is still too expensive for most applications.

The new-fangled radial ply tyres had already arrived - from Michelin - by the mid-1950s. The radically different 'X' was soon optional on many sports and touring cars, and standard on a few. All the effort put into suspension development work began to make sense, for here was a road tyre with precise reactions to match. But it was long life and dry-road handling which benefited; the 'X' was notoriously fickle in wet conditions

59

Backbone-type chassis, and a crude form of independent rear suspension were Standard-Triumph's first thoughts on 1960s engineering. The Spitfire retains this basic layout to this day

Classic 'Forth Bridge' engineering from Daimler for their sports SP250 chassis. Incidentally, this was a close copy of the Triumph TR3 design

Only just room for an engine and
people in the AC Greyhound

Wood for the Marcos in 1961

61

THE POST WAR TOURING CAR

Would this have succeeded as a Standard Vanguard replacement in 1961? At one time, Triumph hoped it would

even George Eyston had fitted discs to his Land Speed Record car 'Thunderbolt' in the 1930s. There were disc brakes on fast aeroplanes in World War Two.

Let's get the facts straight. Jaguar were the first to use proper disc brakes on racing cars (the 'C' Types) in 1952, while Citroen were the first into production (on the DS19, in 1955). In Britain - apart from tiny numbers of sports and racing cars sold by Lotus, Cooper and others - Triumph were first into production with Girling discs on their TR3s, along with a few Jensen 541s which sported Dunlops.

Once the dam had burst, there was no stopping the disc brake revolution. Jaguar soon had four-wheel Dunlop discs on all their cars and by the end of 1958 more than 20 other models had followed Triumph's lead. Discs were so utterly reliable too - there was now no serious remaining brakes problem, and a sports car's progress was never coloured by the reliability of its anchors.

As to the cars themselves, there were important developments. Choice widened, and average prices fell quickly. The Jaguar 2.4, the first Sunbeam Rapiers, the Riley 1.5, the Sunbeam Alpine, the MGA and its Coupe. Even Armstrong-Siddeley tried hard with the rough and ugly 234 sports saloon, and a twin-cam Singer Hunter might have been interesting if financial collapse had not intervened.

The first of the Graber Alvis

Right at the bottom of the scale, cars became more interesting. Alec Issigonis returned from a frustrating mission at Alvis to work wonders with baby Austins and Morrises. The A35 and the Minor 1000 might not look much now, but in 1956 they were almost too good to be true. Better engines, remote-control gearchanges, and higher performance all added up to a new series of rally winners. But it wasn't so much what they were, but what they led to - the Austin-Healey Sprites, and indirectly the new Minis, which made these cars so important. For Issigonis had been spurred on to new heights of genius by the 1956 Suez crises - his new f.w.d. Minis would not arrive until 1959, but were quite accidentally the most promising little sports saloons of all time! But their time would come in the 1960s.

Facing the Mini, Ford could only produce a new Anglia, whose engine would eventually find its way into all manner of racing, sports and touring cars. Harry Webster, at Triumph, was deep into the design of a new Triumph Herald, which was as brave as the Mini, if not as successful.

But the later 1950s were full of interest for us. There was Daimler's SP250, with chassis copied from the TR3, and a remarkable new engine of their own, Ford of Detroit's promising vee-8 Thunderbird, a two-seater in 1954, destined to sink without

Above Armstrong's attempts to get away from the carriage trade with the 236
Below Their 4-cylinder engine that powered the 234

Neat but unsuccessful, the Facellia

Volvo 122 and Sunbeam Rapier, at Crystal Palace on the RAC Rally in 1959

THE POST WAR TOURING CAR

People really did buy a few of these Marcos

much trace in 1958, faster and even faster Porsches, using fewer and fewer VW parts, vast Facel-Vegas from France (with American vee-8s, well before the fashion caught on), and of course the futuristic Citroen DS19, which made every car in the world obsolete when it appeared in 1955.

The times were hard for expensive, small-production cars. Allard outlived their appeal, and disappeared in the late 1950s, Alvis turned into a smooth Graber-bodied saloon, and Frazer Nash at last disappeared in favour of the marketing of Porsches through the same premises. Berkeley caravans tried a tiny motor-cycle engined sports car, but failed in the attempt, and even Aston Martin, with their DB4, seemed determined to go after the rich rather than the sporting.

Volvo had their 122 'Amazon', Lancia their Flaminia, and Chevrolet their rear-engined Corvair. Even the 'Big Six' came alive at last. Triumph made a Vanguard Sportsman (the less said about *that* the better), and Austin a souped up A105. Rootes developed a very ordinary Rapier I into an effective Rapier II and an even more competitive Rapier III. Rumour reached us of the very tuneable little two-stroke Saabs, and of the fast but treacherous Renault Dauphine Gordinis. The approach to making a

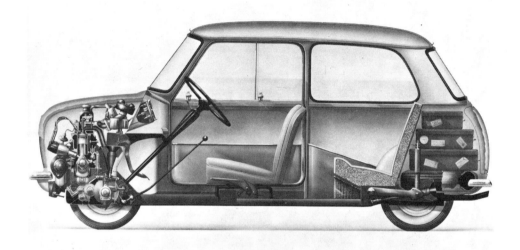

A portent for the future? Alec Issigonis' brilliant little Mini of 1959

sports saloon was changing. Exclusive, hand-built cars were no longer selling, but there was a new and enduring demand for very much faster versions of ordinary cars.

Cars like the Sunbeam Rapiers, the Riley 1.5s and the MGAs were the new favourites. They were not unique - far from it. They were nothing special mechanically - often taking major parts from more ordinary cars. They were built and sold in large numbers. The infuriating thing was that they were potential race and rally winners, in spite of what the purists said.

It was a great shame, but the age of the specialist car was nearly over. Manufacturers like Bristol and AC were not yet prepared to admit this, and had new cars to prove it. The Bristol 406 followed the 404 and 405, while AC's Ace-Bristols, Acecas and Greyhounds were all well-liked. But Lagonda disappeared for a time, Rileys were now no more than special Morrises, and even the MG Magnette was about to be raped in a most unpleasant manner. It was all very depressing - or was it? What potential was there in a Mini? Why was Colin Chapman so interested in the goings on at Ford? Would Jaguar stay out of competition motoring for long? The 1960s might, just might, be as fascinating as ever.

Gunnar Andersson's factory Volvo in the 1961 RAC Rally

Part 5
Sports motoring for all ~
the early 1960s

*T*he retreat of the specialists, but new and interesting cars from the 'Big Five'.
Arrival of the 'GT' saloon, and of the budget-price sporting car. Works entries
in motor sport spur on touring car development. The end of the beginning?

Early in the 1960s, all was bright. We British were prosperous (hadn't Mr
Macmillan already told us so?), our motor industry was once again working flat
out, and some of their new models really sparkled. Many of them were as technically
brave as European competition, and now we even had a few home-grown motorways on
which to try them out. It was true that some renowned builders of sporting machinery
had faded away, but there were some exciting new touring cars on offer which even *we*
could afford.

A marketing revolution was in full flow. Salesmen and whizz-kids had latched on to
the attraction of the budget-priced 'GT' car, and were determined to push this concept as
hard as they could. One had to sort through the mediocre for the good in this little lot,
but a surprising number were good efforts, while some were dramatically successful. No
doubt we will always remember the 1950s for the Triumph TR2s, the Austin-Healey
Sprites and the Jaguars - the early 1960s belong to the Mini-Coopers and the
Lotus-Cortinas. The die-hards just couldn't understand it; it was no longer necessary to
back an exotic car with an exotic badge. The end of the beginning came on the day one
of the Lotus-Cortinas first beat a Jaguar on the tracks.

Saloon car racing and top-class rallying were suddenly big business. In Britain alone
there were works teams from BMC, Ford, Rootes, Triumph, Rover, Vauxhall and Reliant
- all at the same time. Design teams backed up the racing departments' urges for success
and higher performance. Racing tiny saloons stopped being funny and started being
important. The RAC Rally stopped its driving tests and started its forestry marathons.

The Rapier had started this middle-class sporting tradition, and others were quick
to follow. Vauxhall turned their Victors into VX4/90s, Ford their Cortinas into GTs, and
BMC their Minis into Mini-Coopers. So far, so good, and with fine new "2000s" from

THE POST WAR TOURING CAR

Saloon car racing at its most exciting, with the Jaguar 3.8 Mk II

both Rover and Triumph, the interest was well and truly raised, but both BMC and Ford planned to do even better.

The two cars to change the face of British motor sport were the Mini-Cooper S and the Lotus-Cortina. Both were sired by racing teams, both named after the racing cars, and both were intended purely for the sporting scene. The Cooper S happened because John Cooper needed ultimate performance for his 1-litre Formula 3 machines. His basis was the BMC "A" series engine, but by the time the Coventry Engines Branch had finished there was much more special than standard inside. Meantime Cooper had also started the ball rolling with entertaining Mini-Cooper, and it was but a short step from there to marry the very special "S" engine with the Mini-Cooper car. The first was an odd capacity - 1071cc - but Stuart Turner's brave young Finns started to win rallies at once; there would be more, much more, to come with development.

The Lotus-Cortina, at first, was all good engine and all poor development around it! Colin Chapman needed an engine for his new two-seat Elan, found a good base in the Ford 1500 unit, and got *Autocar* Technical Editor Harry Mundy to design him a twin-cam cylinder head to transform its performance. So far, so good, but Chapman next installed the same engine in a Ford Cortina, hastily redeveloped the rear suspension, and persuaded Ford to back it if he made it. The engine was superb, but the rest of the car needed much more development and refinement. Prepared properly, the race cars were winners at once, but it took three years patient effort on Ford's part and persuasion on Lotus to revert to

standard rear springing before the car was a rally winner. But once again, the engine was more significant than the car it powered - the last of these famous engines has only just been made.

By present standards, Cooper S and Lotus-Cortinas were ludicrously cheap. A 1071S cost a mere £695 on announcement (a Mini Super cost £494), while the Lotus-Cortina sold for £1,100 (against £670 for a Cortina 1500 Super). Serious sportsmen could then add as much cost as they liked at the multitude of tuning establishments, who were very happy to supply anything from a special steering wheel to a complete engine conversion!

Somehow it wasn't decent. The purists, to a man, were horrified. Sports touring cars should *look* special, or at least look *different*, but cars like this didn't. You could only tell a VX4/90 from a Victor by its paint scheme, or a Sceptre from a Super Minx by its grille. What would the neighbours say! The purists shouldn't have bothered - the neighbours were too busy queueing up to order this new breed of car to care! It was not only a marketing revolution, but a sales revolution as well. The cars were fast and interesting, and a lot of people wanted to buy. Compared with even five years earlier the response was quite astonishing. Ford's Cortina GT, for instance, which was meant only to be gilt on the 1200's gingerbread, took off as soon as announced. The Willment team started to win saloon car races within weeks, and every British rallying clubman had his new GT as soon as he could find one. Within a year the Cortina GT accounted for one in every four Cortina sales. If ever there was a start to the "GT" boom, this was it. No other

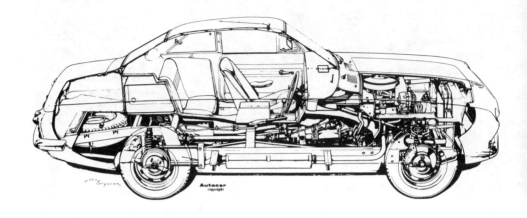

Reliant's Ogle-styled Scimitar — a vast improvement over the original Sabre. This is the later V6 version

Alfa Romeo, BMW 700 Coupe and Panhard — street racing in the 1960 Tour de France

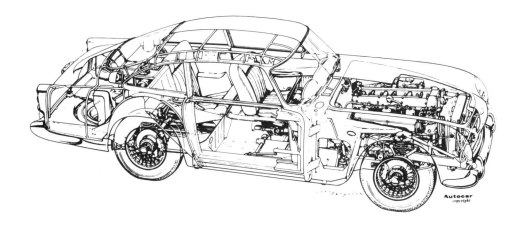

Newport Pagnell's answer to Ferrari — the Aston Martin DB5

Innes Ireland racing an Aston Martin DB4GT

One of the nicest unsuccessful touring cars — AC's 2+2 Greyhound

Pininfarina styling for the Lancia Flaminia Coupe

The Peerless, with Triumph TR mechanicals, and ...

... the Warwick GT developed from it

THE POST WAR TOURING CAR

Daimler's Majestic Major — the last of the true Daimlers

firm was now content until it had a direct competitor.

Against this mass attack, the specialists wilted. Sales dropped, prices rocketed to spread the overheads, and in this desperate spiral more than one make simply disappeared. And yet, there were new contenders who hadn't heard. But did we ever believe in survival for the Gordon GT (later the Gordon-Keeble), even if it did have that splendid Guigiaro-styled body? In the long-life possibilities of a small-engined Facel Vega, the Facellia? In the Bond Equipe (everything the Herald was, without factory service or as much space)? Would a gauche little 2 + 2 Coupe from Wales called the Gilbern last for long, when they bought their bits over the counter from a BMC dealer down the road?

The middle-class GT boom was bad enough, but the specialists must really have suffered when they saw Sir William Lyons' latest creation - the startlingly beautiful E-Type Jaguar - in 1961. It was all very well selling to a market where very high performance could be matched by a high price, but when Jaguar came along with a car, open or closed, that could guarantee 140 mph-plus for only £2,200 that was another myth exploded. E-Types had only two seats at first - the 2 + 2 Coupe would not arrive until 1966 - but the ultra-smooth streamlining, all-independent suspension, and monocoque construction was enough to raise a gleam in any jaundiced writer's eyes. And that splendid closed car had a big shelf behind the seats - big enough certainly for the dog and willing children - didn't that make it a sports saloon too?

But that wasn't all. In Germany the Porsche family had not spent the 1950s merely raking in the profits. The VW-based cars had become more and more specialised as year followed year, but their new car for 1964 was all new. The 911 followed all the

76

Maserati's 3500 GTs

established Porsche tenets - air-cooled, rear-mounted engine, slippery shape, superb transmission, German craftsman-build - but added vastly improved roadholding, a whole lot more performance, and more space to this. Everything from the relatively humble 912 (humble - Ye Gods, even that car did 120mph!) to the fierce 911S had four seats of sorts, and the cars were speedily homologated as "touring cars" for racing purposes.

In the face of this, smaller companies could only evolve improved versions of older designs. The DB4 became the DB4GT, then the DB5. Jensen's 541R put on weight to become the 541S, then lost its looks and added more speed to become the Chrysler-engined CV8. Bristol numbering crept up to 406 (with 2.2-litre engine), and 407 (with a massive 5.1-litre Chrysler vee-8). Mercedes finally threw away their expensive 300SL *and* the stodgy 190SL, replacing both with the pagoda-roof 230SL. From Italy, both Ferrari and Maserati crept up the social and business scale with true production cars instead of lightly-disguised racing coupes. Elsewhere in Italy, Ferruccio Lamborghini decided that Ferrari didn't made good enough cars for him to use, so decided to make his own, while the European-American clan of "mongrels" was joined by Iso and Bizzarrini. On the other hand, Facel Vega went broke in the grandest possible manner, their big American-engined monsters being elephantine, their Facellias not reliable, and the Volvo-engined alternative too late to make any difference. David Brown thought he would revive Lagonda with the DB4-based Rapide, but didn't persist, while Italian coachbuilders got together with Fiat and Lancia to produce some delectable special versions of rather horrid saloons.

Alfa Romoes got better and better - especially when the Giulietta grew up to a

77

Motor Show offerings from Alvis, October 1964. The convertible was much the rarer variant

Fast touring for Herr Pumpernickel — the Mercedes 220SE Coupe

Lancia's dumpy Flavia saloon — the coupes were very desirable

1600cc Guilia and those sleek coupes came along (styling by Bertone - who else?). There was also a new breed of fixed-head coupe, which almost had four seats and almost wasn't a sports car - notable among which were Volvo's new P1800 and Reliant's Scimitar. The P1800 was special because it was originally built (rather badly) by Jensen at West Bromwich, and the Scimitar because it had to out-grow the bad name of its ancestor, the Sabre.

But the most interesting development of all was a sports-touring car boom in the United States, of all places. In the 1950s, only the Corvette and the Thunderbird had shown any signs of being good cars, but by the early 1960s all that had changed. Chevrolet took their reputation in their hands and launched a badly-handling air-cooled flat-six Corvair, which was lousy; this evolved smartly into Corvair Monzas which were splendid. Ford let the Thunderbird grow ... and grow ... and grow, while they beavered away on a new smaller car. The Mustang, when it appeared in April 1964, set the US auto industry by its ears, notched up a million sales in little over two years, and showed that it was remarkably fast on the tracks all over the world. Alan Mann prepared several that won the Tour de France (for Peter Procter in 1964) and many saloon car races in following years. Almost in the sidelines was Studebaker's splendidly fierce Avanti, which became a cult-car as soon as Studebaker went out of business, but right up front, fighting every sale with the European imports, was Chevrolet's Stingray - another American car which did its share of racing over the years.

Further down the excitement-scale there were many important occasions. BMW, who had been rather publicly going broke in 1960, survived excellently with their new

The 1.8-litre Volvo 122S, rugged and reliable. A rally winner just like its predecessor

One of the prettiest of all Alfas — the 1965 Giulia GT

Type 356 Porsche storming the Moistrocca Pass in the 1960 Liege

and advanced BMW 1500s and 1800s, which were to lead all sorts of exciting models in future years. Staid old Peugeot, still making worm-drive cars when every other designer had forgotten about them, suddenly bucked up by announcing a fuel-injection option on their carefully-engineered 404s. Sir William Lyons celebrated the purchase of Daimler by scrapping the ugly old SP250 and approving the Daimler vee-8 engined V8-250 saloon. Lea Francis said they were coming back into car production with their four-seater convertible Lynx, but once we had actually seen the car we were glad they weren't serious, and Rover persevered with their turbine projects in the T4 saloon, long after it was obvious that the concept was too expensive.

By 1964, the emphasis had shifted. Mass-produced sports-saloons were "in" and the select little band of specialists was in trouble. There was no more space for sentiment, no more sympathy for follies. Costs were creeping up, and fine engineering wasn't good enough if not enough of us could afford to buy it. But was there still time for the most splendidly eccentric cars to come through? We already had a vee-8 engined Sunbeam Alpine, but what about the rumoured vee-8 Sceptre? Should we be serious about an Amphicar or what? What plans did Sir William have for Daimler? Leyland for Triumph? Chrysler for Rootes? What did Ford's "Total Performance" philosophy mean to us?

NSU's RO80 — a qualified success?

Part 6
Modern times - mergers and standardisation

A last fling for custom-built machines. Engineering at a new point. Perhaps this will be remembered as a New Golden Age?

At the start of this series, I had to decide what we really meant by a "sports saloon". It was a difficult definition - finally it was necessary to say something like "the sort of closed-car motoring that appeals to an enthusiast". Such cars really ought to have four seats, or be fairly honest 2 + 2s at least, and there should be no doubt the way they performed, handled, or generally behaved.

Even on this broad definition, by the middle of the 1960s, there were far fewer such cars about, and as the old ones died off they were seldom replaced. This was almost entirely due to economic trends. It was a difficult time for an independent car maker to be around - more and more of them disappeared, and their interesting products with them.

The alternative was for them to rush for cover - into the arms of a giant corporation, for the 1960s was the decade of the mergers. When one comes to analyse the slow death of individually-designed sports saloons, British Leyland has a lot to answer for. We once had ruggedly attractive Rileys - after Nuffield, BMC, and after BMC, British Leyland. *Sic transit* ... MG soon turned into a two product concern - nobody in their right-mind would consider a latter-day MG1100 or Magnette. Alvis were swallowed by Rover, which was encouraging, but the two were swallowed by Leyland-Triumph, which wasn't. The Park Ward Alvis was dead on its feet anyway, but Rover's mid-engined four-seater P6BS Coupe could have been one of our finest cars. Alvis would have made them for Rover, the world wanted them, but British Leyland didn't want to harm Jaguar.

As far Jaguar - after the Mk IIs, every succeeding model put on weight, and when the XJ6 appeared in 1968 as a massive and splendidly-engineered flagship there was no

Spen King's exciting mid-engined prototype Rover, which was killed by BLMC

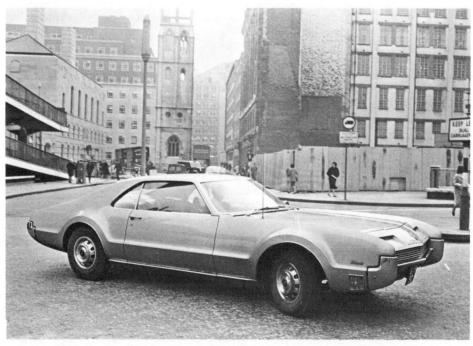

The front-wheel drive Oldsmobile Toronado — a real 'white elephant' from General Motors

Above The Gordon Keeble, with Bertone styling
Below The Gordon Keeble facia

THE POST WAR TOURING CAR

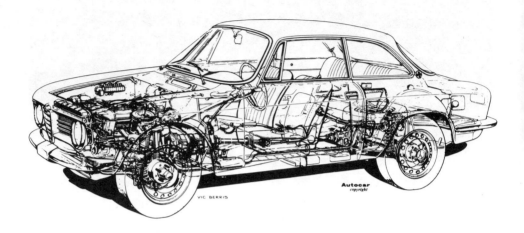

VIC BERRIS

Autocar
copyright

Saloon engineering in a party frock — The Alfa Romeo Giulia Sprint GT. A coupe to us, and a touring car for competition purposes!

hope. Their new 1975 sports car, is really an XJ12 writ small, not nimble, not compact - just dollar-fodder. But what a tragedy - if ever there was an exciting engine looking for a chassis, the XJ 12-cylinder is it.

After the early 1960s, the only new exciting sports saloons were usually expensive. To enjoy "our" sort of motoring it was necessary to be well-heeled. On a very few occasions - as with the MGB GT (almost a 2 + 2, if the children were obliging enough), did the right sort of car come along. Where marketing and product planning took precedence over delicate engineering the product suffered - look at the later Sunbeam Rapiers for proof of that - but occasionally sheer high-spirited enthusiasm got the better of the system, and allowed cars like the Capri to slip through.

Technically there was much of interest in the mid-1960s - and a major talking point was in regard to which, or how many of the road wheels should be driven. Front-wheel drive, of course, needs no additonal public relations apart from its own performance - there are dozens of successful cars in most car-making countries to prove the point - but the discussion centred round the practicable upper-size limits.

One car, a single design exercise, put the cap on that one. General Motors take the credit, astonishingly with nothing less than 7-litre and 8-litre vee-8 engines to supply the urge. Their new car, called an Oldsmobile Toronado at first, but soon joined by a Cadillac cousin, astonished us all in 1965.

There wasn't really *any* good reason why GM should have produced this car at all - front-wheel drive is usually adopted as a space-saver, but GM had plenty of that.

MODERN TIMES — MERGERS AND STANDARDISATION

One of many European-American 'mongrels' — Iso's four-door four-seater Fidia

Apparently they wanted to provide something new for the jaded American car buyer. The trouble was that Toronados looked exactly like any other boring Detroit monster, and since most customers never looked underneath the car anyway the whole idea went off at half-cock.

Another intriguing blind-alley, more significant but less profitable, was Jensen's five-year flirtation with *four*-wheeldrive. I find it interesting, but not surprising, that the FFs have come and gone, the Interceptors remain, and no other car maker has had the nerve, or the need, to emulate Jensen.

Four-wheeldrive, particulary of the Ferguson variety, was supposed to be the ultimate in traction, handling and braking - all very desirable attributes in these crowded days, and all very appropriate to an up-to-date sports saloon. Jensen suffered from the huge extra cost of the Ferguson system, the need to set up every single car before it could be delivered, and the fact that the practical performance didn't seem to be that much more useful than the very sure-footed Jensen Interceptor.

No-one else tried four-wheeldrive in a car - though, of course, there is always the Range Rover, and by my standards that's one of the most enterprising sports saloons in the world. Give me one of those, with a passenger-car engine tune, road tyres instead of knobblies, and stand back. As I've said before - it all depends what you mean ...

Some of the classic touring cars were drawing to the end of their careers, and here I have to pay tribute to such praise-worthy designs as the Graber-styled Alvises, the DB4/5/6 Astons, a few pretty but financially-rocky Glas Coupes, Lancia Flaminias in

THE POST WAR TOURING CAR

Practical sports car — the MGB GT

various shapes and lengths, the attempts by people·like Bristol continuously to uprate their 1940s designs, and the occasional flash of brilliance from mundane companies like Fiat and BMW.

Great big prestige-satisfying monsters like the Facel Vegas finally ran out of customers, and I'm surprised that products like Isos ever found any. The classic touring cars of the 1960s were things like Aston Martin's DBS and DBS V8, Maseratis, Ferraris and even a few Lamborghinis. Money, patience, and a certain place in the world were needed to enjoy this sort of car - and when the car had arrived the bills had not stopped coming either.

For the middle classes, the new cars were few and far between - that is, unless a "GT" or similar model from a member of a vast manufacturing group would do instead. Ford paid Colin Chapman a compliment, and safeguarded their quality reputation, by making Lotus-Cortinas for themselves after 1967, and really excited the competition world with the Escort Twim-Cams and RSs a little bit later.

Rover hid their light under a bushel. Their 2000TC was quick, but not quick enough, and their potentially exciting 3500 was spoiled by a compulsory automatic transmission for the first three years. Triumph offered fuel injection and lots of power in the 2000 structure, but with ageing styling. Rootes insulted the traditionalist by reducing their Humbers to a single model, and basing that on a Hillman Minx. BMC ruined a perfectly good car when they thrust an agricultural 6-cylinder engine into the MGB, and there was no sign of modern Sunbeam Talbot 90s or SS-Jaguars anywhere.

A good attempt from Wales — the Gilbern Genie

To make sports saloons from touring cars, some care and a lot of imagination was needed. British stylists didn't have enough (or their management wouldn't back them) - and in 1967 I felt strongly enough about this to castigate British manufacturers, in *Autocar* for their lack of sport coupes.

From Italy, however, there was good news. Both Lancia and Fiat managed to turn dumpy little saloons into splendidly stylish four-seat coupes with new top-hamper and lines; Alfa Romeo, of course, had been doing it for years. No British company could have been trusted to convert the stubby little Lancia Fulvia saloon into that graceful Coupe, and the way Fiat produced the 124 Sport Coupe from the basis of the square-rigged 124 saloon was nothing short of miraculous. The sort of coupes this country produce are Firenzas from Vivas or Rapiers from Hunters.

One had to admire Rolls-Royce for their efforts with the new Silver Shadow, even if it had taken ten years to do, the handling was not up to much, and the price was quite out of the ordinary, though Rover's own vee-8 engine was probably more significant to the likes of us. Rover, of course, grafted the ex-Buick vee-8 engine into the old 3-litre cars to give it a new lease of life. Too many people had written off the 3-litre as stodgy and dull - they never bothered to find out that the 3.5 was neither.

One has to look back wistfully at the projects that might have been pressed on, or the design studies that were killed by timid directors. Apart from Rover's splendid mid-engined car, there were the rear-engined Sunbeams and Singers that never had the engines they deserved, the front-wheel drive and mid-engined sporting prototypes which

Rare beast — the 4-wd Jensen FF

The car that killed Marcos — the Triumph PI-engined Mantis, styled by Dennis Adams

Elegance and nearly four seats from Lotus — the Elan Plus 2

Striking and successful, Fiat's 124 Sport Coupe

THE POST WAR TOURING CAR

The Reliant Scimitar GTE

BMC made from time to time and the fast-back/estate bodies on Triumph 2000 and Jaguar Mk II body shells which appeared in public after the sponsors had taken flight.

Occasionally, very occasionally, an independent has produced a four-seater. Gilbern's Genie, later named the Invader, was lamentably under-developed and over priced, but a good stylish effort to follow their dumpy little 1800. Marcos never aspired to a four-seater until they were on the slide to bankruptcy (and when we saw the result we wondered why they had bothered) and AC missed a glorious chance when they kept their 15 foot 7-litre vee-8 428 as a two-seater; true, there was an upholstered shelf behind the driver, but with 19 inches of headroom nobody took it seriously.

The really successful effort came from Lotus, whose timelessly elegant Elan Plus Two was only let down by is distressing reliability record. At first Colin Chapman priced it at no more than £1,672 in component form, for which we could have 120mph performance, refinement, superb handling, and that indefinable something of a Lotus badge on the nose. It was the right car, expertly marketed, and one which no other British firm could match. Aston Martin, AC, Jaguar and the like were all on their "large engine" kick, and the mass-produced competition such as MGB GTs and Triumph GT6s (the latter only a two-seater) could not compete.

Before the end of the 1960s there were occasionally flashes of design brilliance, as some brave design team gripped economic facts by the throat and attempted to beat the trends. Whatever the VW accountants may now say, a classic car enthusiast of the future will probably drool over his NSU Ro80. Apart from its rather horrid three-speed

Lamborghini's beautiful four-seater Espada

clutchless gear-change the Ro80 was a splendidly advanced and satisfying machine to drive. So far it has been the only multi-rotor Wankel-engined car to be made in any numbers in Europe, but sadly it has been no commercial success. The cost of spares in this country is ludicrously high, and I doubt if the car will ever live down its reputation for eating its own engine seals at regular, and premature intervals, even though the problem is long since solved.

The little company in Tamworth - Reliant - also started we scribes twittering in 1968 when they launched their Ogle-styled Scimitar GTE, where the merits of a racehorse *and* a load carrier (see their advertising to note how appropriate this is) were combined. The sporting estate was a very attractive way of pleasing modern enthusiasts, and it is surprising how few have copied the layout. Volvo tried with their 1800ES, which was only a two-seater, but BMW with their 2002 Touring, Lotus with the new Elite, Ford with their Capri II and Renault with their 15s and 17s are much more important disciples of this layout.

But what of the future? With companies as large as British Leyland struggling even to survive, let alone make big profits, we shouldn't expect them to pander to an enthusiast's whims. Whether we admit it or not, there are fewer and fewer of us about - fewer, at least prepared to spend money on this particular type of car. Perhaps in future years, we may look back on the 1950s and 1960s with affection. Perhaps, in time, we will begin to call them the New Vintage Years?

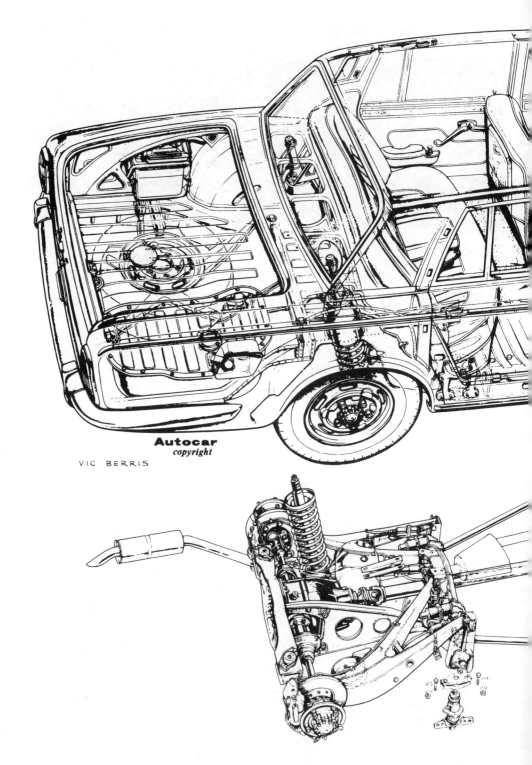

Autocar
copyright

VIC BERRIS

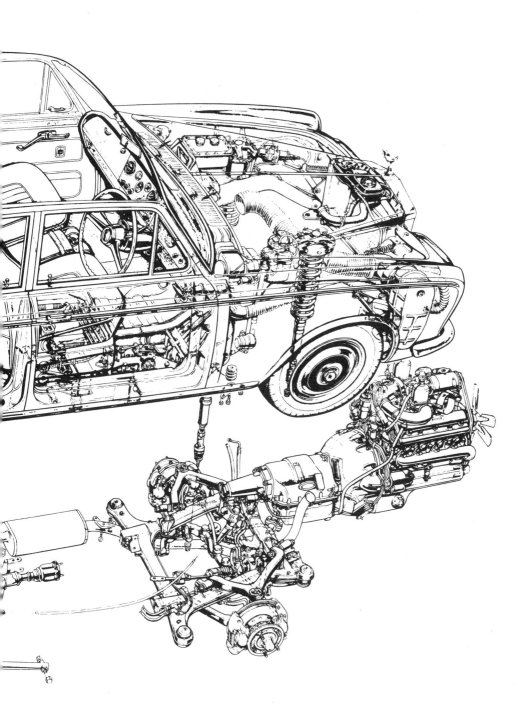

Perhaps the grandest of all — the Rolls-Royce Silver Shadow, first seen in 1965

Some might say the Porsche Turbo was excessive, others a means to an end

Part 7
Looking back and looking forward

*S*umming up. Is the 'Classic Car' losing the battle? There are depressing signs that this is so. Should we enjoy our motoring while we can? Who should be saluted by posterity? What are the enthusiast's prospects?

I think we would all agree that for a car to be accepted as a sports saloon, it would have to be that important bit 'different'. It would have to be better than average either in looks, in its engineering and performance, and certainly in its marketing intentions.

On that score I don't think there is any doubt that there are designers and salesmen around today who would still dearly love to sell that sort of new car to us. Their trouble, now as never before, is the pressure of costs and production economics. This is not merely confined to cars either - special trains with special fittings have nearly disappeared, airline flights are becoming more and more standardised, luxury travel by liners has disappeared - and all because the cost of doing this sort of thing has rocketed.

Put in football terms, we just don't have a 'second division' any more. Even as late as the 1940s, the 'Big Six' - Austin, Morris, Ford, Rootes, Standard and Vauxhall - were our 'first division', with lots of respected independents like Rover, Jaguar, Daimler, Armstrong-Siddeley or Jowett trading away in the 'second division'. But what now? Our 'first division' is really our only division. Take away the Big Four of British Leyland, Ford, Vauxhall and Chrysler from the lists and what is left? The rump of the British Industry relies on firms like Reliant and Lotus to stay afloat. A measure of the situation is that, after British Leyland, Lotus and Reliant make counter-claims to being the second-largest British-owned car makers! How times have changed.

Even in the golden days, there was quite a lot of mechanical rationalistion between bread-and-butter cars and the sports saloons they supported, but because this was hidden under attractive coachwork we didn't mind. A Sunbeam-Talbot 90, for instance, shared its engine and transmission with the Humber Hawk, an MG Magnette with other

THE POST WAR TOURING CAR

Sunbeam-Talbot 90 cutaway — a 'nice' car

Wolseleys and Austins, and a Jensen 541 with the A135 Austin carriage which took the mayor to and from his dignified town hall.

What made all the difference, eventually, was that it simply wasn't 'on' to spend capital on a special body for a special car. The end would have been delayed for some time if unit-construction structures had not arrived so steadily. In North America, where the separate chassis frame is still going strong, Detroit has often been able to disguise one basic body behind a mass of new skin panels and decoration. The best we can do in Europe is to make coupes out of saloons: some, like Fiat, do better than others. General Motors succeeded with the Opel Manta but failed with the Vauxhall Firenza. Ford, apart from Granada Ghias, didn't bother, nor did British Leyland.

Even twenty years ago, when I started work at Jaguar, I vividly recall Sir William Lyons' annual 'pep-talk' to his staff and technicians. Sir William was as anxious as anyone to maintain the individuality of his cars, but pointed out that *even then* the tooling cost of a new body shell would be more than one million pounds! Not many years later it would cost around £50,000 to make major changes to the ventilation system of a Triumph saloon. In 1975, proper tooling for the nose-job on an Escort RS2000 or Vauxhall Firenza would exceed the quarter-million mark.

Weight saving, safety provisions, the needs of quantity production, and good old-fashioned inflation account for this. It is simply not possible for a large company to make money with slow-selling vehicles. The famous London taxi-cab is no sports saloon (or is

In the same vein an Alvis TA21

it?), but in production figures it makes a good example. For years Austin, and later BMC, persevered with the cab, selling a few thousand every year, but British Leyland couldn't wait to rid themselves of the burden. They still provide bits and pieces to Carbodies Limited, who have always erected the distinctive body shells, but Carbodies now assemble the whole vehicle. When the old taxi fades away, a new design is not likely to be produced.

With metal bodywork, one either builds millions, spending millions on preparation and tooling and mechanised production, or one builds very few, where hand-beating and craftsman-construction is everything. Aston Martin were one of the last of the specialists, and Jensen are just deceased.

How, indeed, can Bob Jankel's Panthers (he has taken the Monica under his wing), and the like look forward to the future? Handwork in the 1980s is something that may be hard to justify. It may be even harder to find the men to do the job.

Glassfibre bodies, on the other hand, will probably fill the gap. There is simply no way that quantity production of glassfibre shells can be arranged - a lengthy lay-up process and curing time ensures that - and after Colin Chapman's attempts to tame the vagaries of a glassfibre monocoque with his first Elite there is no scramble to emulate him.

Renault, at least, have shown that with a large enough factory, modern methods, and the right sort of design, more than 20,000 bodies of one type can be made in a year.

THE POST WAR TOURING CAR

The mid-seventies 'sports touring' car, the limited production Ford Escort RS2000

More than that would require duplicated facilities, tools and labour force. And by then production volume would be approaching Jaguar's level, where a fully-tooled series of sheet-steel monocoques is completely justified.

One reason it is so much more difficult to provide for a specialised car these days is that the *general* level of demand has increased so much. The general expectation, and need, for sales volumes, has risen so far that a re-incarnated 1930s or 1940s production manager would stare in amazement.

One hundred SS-Jaguars every week was a good production rate in 1939, whereas eight or ten times that number is possible now. Colin Chapman sold nearly 1,000 of the first Elite between 1959 and 1963. He now needs to sell more than that number of £7,500 Elites in the new fashion every year to keep his factories in business. How often did Aston Martin sell more than ten cars every week in the 1950s and 1960s? And how many would be needed to make Newport Pagnell viable today? The gap between what is now an economic rate of manufacture and what is actually a potential sales figure becomes progressively more difficult to marry up. Jensen took nearly three years to build the first 1,000 Vignale-styled Interceptors, and by 1973 (before the energy crisis struck) were building 1,500 a year, and planning on 2,500 by 1976. Even that, with the Jensen-Healey would not have been enough.

Companies like Rolls-Royce, who can make between 3,000 and 4,000 cars a year, charge the earth for them, and still feel confident enough to launch the £29,000

The Renault 30TS has become one of the more familiar European motorway 'cruisers'

Camargue, have decades of prestige to lean on. Bristol, who made around 150 cars a year from the 1940s to the present day, have a particular product and a particular clientele to back them. But will there ever be radically new Rolls-Royce or Bristol models?

It was not just a company's inability to make the cars either. Even when a car was exciting, attractive, and in great favour with press and public, the customers - you and I - were not actually battering on the doors to buy them. Coming forward to the 1960s both BMC and Lotus needed to sell 1,000 of their rally-specials (Cooper S and Lotus-Cortina respectively) every year to achieve homologation for competition purposes. Both struggled. Lotus made only 500 in 1964 and still got homologation approval! This improved to 1,100 in 1965, but when the cars competed under the later Group One rules (5,000 a year) there was widespread, and justified disbelief. BMC certainly couldn't sell 1,000 Cooper S cars every year until their racing and Monte Carlo Rally wins had clinched the publicity. By then they were Group One approved - and nobody believed that either!

Over the years, there have been many outstanding cars, and many disappointments. It is idle to wonder what the world of motoring would have been like without the effects - social and financial - of the Second World War. But just suppose ..... just suppose?

Without a war, the world would not be the place it is today, a truism if ever there was one. However, the 1940s and 1950s, as far as the motor industry is concerned, would have been very different. It is a fact that the war made a dramatic difference to general

101

THE POST WAR TOURING CAR

Still it's grace, space and pace — the Jaguar XJ5.3C

price levels, and to Government taxation policies. The specialist motor industry never really recovered from the much higher prices that obtained after 1945, prices made worse by the imposition of purchase tax, at a double rate for a time in some cases.

Without a war, some cars and companies would have survived much longer. Even at their production levels they would not have suffered the sheet steel shortages that could only be circumvented by allocating cars for export. One mourns companies like Lagonda, whose 1939 LG6s and vee-12s were splendid machines able to match the best from Rolls-Royce and Daimler in many ways; their day had yet to come. On the other hand, Riley would certainly have become Nuffield-ised much quicker than in fact they did, Triumph might never have been taken over by a large concern like Standard, and David Brown would never have been around to buy Aston Martin when in fact he did. There would have been no convenient Air Ministry 'shadow factories' easily to be turned into car-making halls. Renault would never have been nationalised, VW's fortunes might have been very different, the genius of Colin Chapman would probably not have flowered at the right time. Vehicle styling and engineering, much affected as it was by military developments, would have veered off on a different track. Brooklands might have survived, Donington certainly would have. Of Silverstone and MIRA there would be no trace. Is it even worth saying 'just suppose?'.

In Britain, the great disappointments have all been tempered by economic disaster or a change of management. At the time of writing, several companies making fine cars

The first of the 'new generation' Citroens — this is a CX 2200

have failed, financially, and inevitably there will be more. The tragedy of Aston Martin was that they had consistently sold cars for less than they cost, and refused to rationalise by using more standard parts, even where these might not have been noticed. Daimler could most certainly have survived without take-over by Jaguar. After all, they were part of the large BSA group, and with a healthy military and public passenger transport business to back up the fine cars, their future was not in doubt. *That* sell-out was due to BSA's then-management not being sufficiently car minded. Rationalisation with Jaguar soon killed off two of the finest vee-8 engines yet designed in Britain.

Armstrong-Siddeley's biggest mistake was in trying to beat Jaguar at their own game, but without their production capacity, enthusiastic public, and potential sales volumes. The Sapphire was a splendid car which outdid the Mark 7 Jaguar on most fronts. What followed - the lumpy 234s and 236s - is best forgotten. By the end of the 1950s, Bristol-Siddeley with all their government-financed aerospace work did not *need* to make cars any more. When the directors lose their enthusiasms, and there are options, an affair of the heart like a sporting car usually suffers.

I have always classified Bristol as a great disappointment. Its chroniclers will no doubt howl with rage, but the fact is that Bristol have never developed a new model, except by progressive refinement of a basically pre-war design, since their first Type 400. Once again this has been a question of a large and diverse corporation losing interest in a side-line. Bristol when owned by the aircraft company could certainly have afforded a

103

THE POST WAR TOURING CAR

Lotus Cars had joined the luxury 'touring' car producers with the Elite

new model; Anthony Crook's concern cannot.

I was sorry to see that Jowett's enterprise came to nothing. That the Javelin might not have been so rapturously received if it had come from a more likely source is an interesting theory. The Bradford management had done it once, but could they have done it again?

Other failures were predictable. Facel Vega, Gordon-Keeble, and Iso because as Euro-American mongrels they could not establish a predigree. Lancia (thankfully rescued by Fiat) because they were family-controlled and under-financed. Pegaso because they knew nothing about the motoring business when they started, and no more when they finished. Borgward, on the other hand, were very unlucky.

The side-alleys and still-born cars are of interest, but are they of significance? How seriously should we now look back on Ferguson's four-wheel drive experiments, and the only cars sold (Jensen FFs) with the system fitted? Apart from its acknowledged traction in certain conditions, was it really worth all that expense and complication? The Ferguson cars themselves were in reality much less satisfactory than their road tests published would have us believe. Their flat-four engines were unnecessary, and their slow-pulsing anti-lock braking an inefficient bore. So many people, car firms, police forces, and others tried the cars. So few actually ordered examples for themselves.

What of the Wankel? Apart from the fuel consumption problems and emission-limiting complications which are now well-known, a Wankel engine is now

The Jaguar XJS is a triumph of value for money. It runs quite well too!

subjectively a very fine machine. Take away the problem of actually affording to run an Ro80 or a Mazda RX4, and you see some most sybaritic motoring hiding underneath.

The facts of motoring life have changed so drastically since the Yom Kippur War of 1973, and the economic use of the oil weapon which followed it, that all our expectations of motoring pleasure have had to be changed. From now on, the accent must be on fuel conservation, attention to aerodynamic improvements, and attempts to raise reliability standards. Peformance, tyre burning and sheer motoring enjoyment must take a submissive back seat.

Be that as it may, the 'sports saloon' enthusiast can still look around and find up-to-date cars to interest him. To hide his enthusiasm (almost) behind a workmanlike exterior, he will probably lean towards the new breed of high-performance estate cars (Lancia call theirs precisely that anyway!) though the load carrying function of cars like the latest Lotus, Reliant, Renault or Ford is not thought likely to influence sales.

If he has the money to back him, the latest in Porsches (the Turbo?), in Citroens (the CX), Rovers, Jaguars, Mercedes, Ferraris, Lamborghinis and the like, are lined up awaiting his custom.

But even if the wherewithal is restricted, the general standard of motor cars has risen so much in the last decade that his only concession will be to individuality. Anyone happily taking delivery of an Alfa Giulietta in the early 1950s could scorn many of Europe's bread-and-butter saloons. An XK120 bought in 1949 or 1950 was so much quicker and more exciting than almost anything else on the market that we marvel how the others sold cars at all. Even a Sunbeam Rapier was loads better than its related Hillman Minx. The touring car of the 1970s is generally of a very high standard. We would be silly to emulate pundits of the 1930s who thought that motoring had already reached its peak, but we can at least take heart from a competent base level. Not everyone can aspire to an Escort RS2000 in 1976 (even if you accept it as a sports saloon) - less powerful Escorts handle as well, and even go quite briskly. A humble Fiat, Renault, Volkswagen or Austin is not the pudding it once might have been.

Before winding up the narrative, there are several outstanding designs to which I must pay homage. I must start, as I suspect I must end, with Jaguar. It is nearly thirty years ago, now, but I can still recall the thrill, the excitement, and even a touch of disbelief with which we all greeted Sir William's XK120 sports car and its all new XK twin-cam engine. This, more than any other, must have convinced the world of motoring that there was more in engine design than super-tuning a push-rod lump. The XK engine was the world's first twin-cam to go into quantity production, and it was many years before the sales build-up was overtaken by Alfa-Romeo.

After the Jaguar, Alfa-Romeo with their Giuliettas (and later the Giulias) come next. They took Jaguar's philosophy one stage further and proved that two of everything is not necessarily difficult to maintain. The Alfa cars, like the XK Jaguars, are still going, in one way or another.

Citroen's shark-nosed DS19 signalled the end and the beginning of two ages of motoring. Before 1955 that sort of technical innovation was ignored; after that it was embraced. The DS19 was so advanced, and so far ahead of its time, that the rest of the motor industry took years to catch up; Citroen's tragedy was that they then sat back and let this happen.

After Citroen, Alec Issigonis. His front-wheel drive theory was not entirely new, but the concept of a transverse engine and incredibly compact body was brilliant. Issigonis has noted copyists all over the world; those companies who have not fallen into line are probably still making up their minds.

I look upon the Mercedes 300SL as proof that racing still could improve the breed, even if it didn't bring many profits. On the other hand I look on Porsches as a good case of racing being made to prove an already agreed breed. Early racing Porsches were made to use VW parts because Porsche's family decreed it.

I gave a nod to Ferrari for daring to sell complicated vee-12 engines in the first place, but I bow down to Sir William Lyons *again* for daring to sell them in large numbers. I salute Colin Chapman for the way his Lotus cars have outlived a very doubtful reliability image, for the way the company built itself up from nothing, and for the way they seem determined to be completely independent sporting-car manufacturers, against all obvious odds.

In spite of the tone of much of this narrative, and the way we have seen company after company disappearing, I hope we have not reached the end of an era. I hope and believe that in ten years time there will be more to be added to this story. For whatever our masters may legislate against us, the urge to motor for enjoyment will take a long time to die, and the people who make cars to sell us know it..

The new Rover 3500 will allow no-one to mistake it for its ancestors

Makes; Who started, and who remain?

These were the *marques* listed by *The Autocar* and *The Motor* at the end of 1946:

AC
Allard
Alvis
Armstrong Siddeley
Austin
Bentley (Owned by Rolls-Royce)
Bristol
Daimler
Ford
Frazer Nash
Healey
Hillman (Owned by Rootes)
HRG
Humber (Owned by Rootes)
Invicta
Jaguar
Jensen
Jowett
Kendall (This 'people's car' never went into production)
Lagonda
Lanchester (Owned by Daimler)
Lea-Francis
MG (Owned by Nuffield)
Morgan
Morris (Owned by Nuffield)
Riley (Owned by Nuffield)
Rolls-Royce
Rover
Singer
Standard
Sunbeam-Talbot (Owned by Rootes)
Triumph (Owned by Standard)
Vauxhall
Wolseley (Owned by Nuffield)

THE POST WAR TOURING CAR

Aston-Martin cars were not then in production, though development of post-war products was under way.

Five years later, at the 1951 Earls Court Motor Show, the following important changes had already occurred:

Austin, and the Nuffield Group were preparing to merge.
Invicta had disappeared.
Marauder and **Paramount** had appeared in the lists.

In another five years, at the 1956 Earls Court Motor Show, there had been further changes:

Healey had disappeared, to be replaced by **Austin-Healey** in the BMC line-up.
Sunbeam-Talbot had disappeared, replaced by **Sunbeam,** still Rootes-owned.
Singer was now owned by Rootes.
HRG, Jowett, Lanchester and **Lea-Francis** had all disappeared.
Lotus had joined the lists.

In 1961, at the Earls Court Motor Show, there were further changes:

Allard, Armstrong-Siddeley had disappeared, with **Frazer-Nash** about to join them.
Reliant and **Vanden Plas** (an 'invented' BMC *marque*) were new in the lists.

Five years later, in 1966, there had been minor changes:

Lagonda and **Standard** had gone.
Bond and **Gilbern** had been added.
Jaguar and **Daimler** had merged.

In 1971, the Earls Court scene showed this:

The British Leyland merger now embraced **Austin, Daimler, Jaguar, MG, Mini, Morris, Rover, Triumph, Vanden Plas** and **Wolseley.**
Alvis, Austin-Healey, Riley and **Singer** had all gone.

In 1976 the ranks at the final Earls Court show were further deplated:

Clan, Gilbern, Jensen and **Marcos** - all Grand Touring Cars - had gone. **Humber, Sunbeam** and **Wolseley** had all been rationalised out of existence. **AC** were in suspended animation - not having sold any cars since 1973.
There were two new marques - **Panther** and **Princess.**
Hillman, when the **Hunter** is withdrawn, will be the next to go.

Those taking part

Any trend is made up of many tiny incidents. Any survey must only touch on many individual stories. Many of the fascinating details that have influenced modern sports saloon design can be credited to a single car or company.

In Europe, at least, there have been dozens of *marques* all with their own little story to tell. What follows, in many cases, tells just the bare bones of their progress since 1945:

AC   *Cars made at Thames Ditton*   *First car sold in 1909*

This tiny company greeted post-war years with an outdated design. The 2-litre saloon was smart but mechanically un-inspired, with its six-cylinder engine dating from 1919, and its pre-war type beam axle chassis. It was one of the last two British models to be built with a beam front axle (the Ford Popular was the other).

The Hurlocks who control AC astounded us all by productionising John Tojeiro's Bristol-engined sports racing car, giving it the venerable AC engine, and calling it the Ace. With every succeeding engine transplant the car became fiercer, faster and more competitive. Ace-Bristols came next, then Ace-Zephyrs, and finally Cobras, the largest having 7-litre Ford vee-8 engines.

There was the 2 + 2 Greyhound, which was virtually a long-wheelbase Aceca with unique chassis and details.

After the 7-litre Cobras AC reverted to building a very few AC428 coupes with Frua bodies, but these have been dropped. At the time of writing the new AC 3000, with its mid-mounted Ford vee-6 engine, has not yet entered production.

111

THE POST WAR TOURING CAR

Alfa-Romeo   *Cars made in Milan Italy*   *First car sold in 1910*

Like Renault, Alfa-Romeo is a very successful nationalised concern.

Up to the war their machines put engineering before money value; afterwards the process was reversed. Not that a post-war Alfa was nasty. Every post-war car has had one or other twin-cam engine - even the Romeo vans are so equipped. In 1934 (their best post-depression year) they built a mere 699 cars; production exceeded 10,000 in 1956, and 20,000 in 1958.

The little 1.3-litre Giulietta arrived in 1954, and the bigger-engined Giulia in 1962. These cars, and their successors have been powered by a huge variety of 1.3, 1.6, 1.8 and 2.0 litre engines. Alfas have raced and rallied with distinction all over the world.

Large cars - the 1900 became the 2000, in turn replaced by the 2600s - have not succeeded as well.

Alfa's latest and successful venture is the front-wheel-drive Alfasud project, with cars made in great numbers in the new Naples factories.

Allard   *Cars made in Clapham*   *First car (Allard Special) made in 1935*

Sid Allard was a motor trader who liked motor sport. His first special was an amalgam of steel tubing (his own), vee-8 engine (Ford) and GP Bugatti body (from a write-off). There were a few, very few, Allard Specials sold before 1939.

Allards were properly in production from 1946. All had tubular chassis, and split-beam transverse-leaf front suspension. There were body styles in profusion, from stark two-seater sports to bulbous P1 saloons. Sid won the Monte Carlo Rally in his own P1 in 1952, and sales prospered. The most popular Allards were racers with vast Cadillac vee-8s - many still being used in America.

Fashions changed, and cars like the XK120 killed the big Allards. The smaller, more delicate Palm Beaches also failed because TR2s and Austin-Healeys were better.

The last of several hundred Allards was built at the end of the 1950s, when the company turned to making Ford performance conversions and marketing superchargers - plus, of course, remaining as prosperous motor traders.

Alvis   *Cars made in Coventry*   *First car sold in 1920*

There are those who think 1930s Alvises - the 3.5 and 4.3-litre cars in particular - were better than Derby Bentleys. They were not built again after 1945.

Alvis prospered by making aero-engines, and latterly versatile military vehicles. Cars became an elegant but minor side-line. The post-war TA models were pre-war 12/70s reworked and updated. The only true post-war product was the 3-litre, first shown as an 85bhp saloon in 1950, and last built as a 150bhp Park Ward Coupe in 1967. The TC/TD/TE/TF series was never in the van of technical development, and eventually fell behind Jaguar and others in the performance race. They enjoyed a brief period of competition activity in the 1950s.

Their most famous non-event was in employing Alec Issigonis for a period in the 1950s to design a brand-new 3½-litre vee-8 engined car, which actually had the first Moulton-Hydrolastic-type suspension. The car worked, and worked well, but capital to build it was not made available.

THOSE TAKING PART

Alvis will remain famous for these saloons and coupes, but there were also a few sports cars and drophead coupes from time to time. The company was taken over by Rover in 1965, and were to have produced the mid-engined Rover P6BS Coupe. Rover-Alvis were then purchased by Leyland-Triumph in 1967 and the project was killed.

Armstrong-Siddeley   *Cars made in Coventry*   *First car sold in 1902 (as a Siddeley)*

Armstrong-Siddeleys were close behind Rolls-Royce and Daimler in the carriage-trade business up to 1939. Thereafter they opted out. Post-war products, announced in the week the Nazis surrendered, were based on a 16hp chassis. There were Lancasters, Hurricanes, Whitleys and Typhoons, all uninspired with 2.3-litre six-cylinder engines.

The Sapphires which followed, in 1952, were aimed at the Jaguar Mk VII and Alvis market, succeeding admirably. Their 3.4-litre engines were later copied by Rootes for Super Snipes (in exchange Armstrong-Siddeley built Alpines at first). Sapphires and Star Sapphires were good cars, much better than the gawky 234s and 236s which followed. The 234 was a rough and rorty disaster, and the 236 only appealed to Armstrong die-hards. A-S were taken over by Bristol for their aero-engined interests, car production languished, and ceased altogether in 1960.

Aston Martin   *Cars made at Feltham, later Newport Pagnell*   *First car sold in 1922*

The Newport Pagnell firm was Christmas 1974's most newsworthy disaster. It was not the first time the company faced liquidation. Pre-war Astons were few, expensive, and splendid sports cars.

David Brown, the industrialist, bought Astons *and* Lagonda in 1947, married the two and sponsored the DB2 with its Bentley-designed Lagonda engine. There were DB2s, DB2/4s, DB Mk 3s, DB4s, DB5s and DB6s all in the same 2-seat or 2 + 2 seat coupe vein, before the much larger DBSs and DBS-V8s arrived in the later 1960s. Only the Aston Martin V8 remained in 1974, a big loss-maker, like most of its predecessors. No-one could make the company pay, and even the Government recognised this.

The company's 'vintage' period was the 1950s, with more and yet more prestigious sports racing wins; these culminated in a Le Mans victory *and* the Sports Car Championship in 1959. After this there was nothing left but to retire.

The Aston mystique remains, though only the engine design deserved the lavish praise. The company's basic problem was that it never charged enough money for the cars it made, and couldn't sell more at the prices it charged - a sure recipe for financial disaster. Let us hope the new owners have better luck.

Bentley   *Post-war cars made at Crewe*   *First car sold in 1921*
First Rolls-built car sold in 1933

The post-war Bentley was only a name. No more than that and a winged badge remained of W.O.'s vintage masterpieces. The Mk VI, its sister Silver Dawn Rolls-Royce, and the R Type development were the first Rolls-sponsored cars with standard steel bodies. After this very few coachbuilt machines were erected on Crewe chassis and mechanicals.

113

THE POST WAR TOURING CAR

Mechanical progress was slow. The old engine, dating back in its roots to the 1920s, was made in 4¼, 4½ and 4.9-litre form until 1959. It was then replaced by a Cadillac-inspired 6.2-litre vee-8 (now 6.75-litre). Separate-chassis R Types were replaced by separate-chassis S Types in 1955, and by the current monocoque T Series in 1965. Bentley have been interested only in high-price saloons and their derivatives in post-war years; their continued existence is now an anachronism as they are mechanically identical to Rolls-Royce Shadows and identically priced. Very few are made.

The only semi-sporting cars were the series of Continentals and Flying Spurs built on R and S Type mechanicals in the 1950s.

BMC - Mini   *Cars made at Cowley and Longbridge*   *First cars sold in 1959*

Alec Issigonis returned from Alvis to take over the BMC engineering effort in the mid-1950s, and set about making a new small car. The Austin and Morris Minis were conceived to beat off possible petrol crises, and were astonishingly advanced - re-introducing tranverse engines and front-wheel-drive to the British public.

Superb handling, controllability, and clever packaging screamed out for more performance, which arrived in the shape of the 997cc Mini-Coopers in 1961, and the Mini-Cooper S in 1963 (1071cc) and 1964 (970 and 1275cc). Coopers and Cooper Ss won races and rallies all over the world, including the Monte Carlo Rally on three occasions (plus another 'disqualified' win) in the 1960s.

Now the Mini is an art form of its own, with a name of its own. Coopers became uncompetitive in 1968, and disappeared altogether in 1971.

Well over four million of all Minis have now been made.

BMW   *Cars made in Bavaria, West Germany*   *First sold in 1928*

The pre-war BMW 327s and 328s were among the world's best sports cars, but the company never regained its factories as the Russian armies had over-run it. The ugly two-stroke Watrburgs are made there now!

Starting from scratch in Munich, BMW made small numbers of big-engined cars in the 1950s, the sleek 507 sports car being by far their best effort.

Financial disaster was staved off in 1961 by the new 1500 saloons, which developed rapidly, until the 2000TI became a race winner. Smaller but fast BMWs followed, with six-cylinder saloons and coupes in some profusion.

BMW now hold six per cent of the German market and market a bewildering array of models, each powered by one or other of the single-cam engine family.

There are also splendidly expensive flat-twin motorcycles, much favoured by police forces of the world.

Bond   *Cars made in Preston, Lancs*   *First car sold in 1963*

The company's first products were fragile little three-wheelers, with air-cooled motorcycle engines. A link was forged with Standard-Triumph in 1963. The company's first four-wheeler, the Equipe GT, had Triumph Herald mechanicals and much of the body structure, with Bond styling of a coupe body. Later models inherited the Spitfires's 1300cc engine, while there was a 2-litre Vitesse-engined car built on similar lines. The cars carried Triumph's mechanical guarantee, but were expensive. Bond eventually fell into difficulties and were taken over by Reliant. Car production ceased in 1971.

The Bond Bug 3-wheeler was really a Reliant styled for the Carnaby Street brigade, and has now been dropped.

Bristol   *Cars made in Bristol*   *First car sold in 1946*

Founded immediately after the war, in liaison with the Aldington family, the company took possession of all the BMW 328 and allied technology. The first Bristol, the 400, was really an updated BMW, and its chassis has been updated but basically unchanged, ever since.

Bristol engines of 2-litres have been tuned to more than 150bhp, and powered cars as diverse as ACs, Cooper single-seaters, and various Frazer-Nash models.

The 401s and 403s raced and rallied with success, the 404 was their most gallant commercial failure. Bristol joined the 'fit American' brigade with the Chrysler vee-8 powered 407 in 1961 and their two-door saloons evolved into gentleman's carriages. There has been no competition activity since then, and over the years the car has been progressively updated. In 1976 a Bristol still broadly based on the old 400 chassis design now has a 5.9-litre Chrysler vee-8 engine, and is called the 603. It seems highly unlikely that there will ever be a brand-new Bristol car.

Chevrolet   *Cars made in Detroit, USA and elsewhere*   *First car sold in 1911*

For the most part Chevrolet, just one part of the mighty General Motors empire, has made huge quantities of Detroit iron. Occasionally some interesting designs have slipped through the corporate filters, and in recent years the engineering development staff have carried out much 'back door' competition effort.

The 2-seat Corvette has been America's only true sports car for some years. Chevrolet engineers produced the flat-six, rear-engined, air-cooled Corvair in 1959, which was a rigid shock to dealers and customers alike. Pilloried by the Nader anti-GM campaign regarding its peculiar handling, the Corvair was a financial loser to GM (who could afford it). Their Monza versions, some with supercharged engines, are of great interest to collectors.

Recently Chevrolet have produced compacts like the Camaro, and the latest sporting developments like the Monte Carlo are much more suited to European tastes.

Citroen   *Cars made in various factories in France*   *Cars first sold in 1919*

Since 1945, Citroen have never produced a dull car. Their 'traction avant' range carried on successfully until 1955, when it was replaced by the startlingly advanced DS19. In the meantime the 2CV had been in use since 1948, and is even more appropriate to the frugal 1970s.

The DS19 was a complete design revolution - for Citroen and the automotive business - with its power-assisted everything, self-levelling hydro-pneumatic suspension, front-wheel-drive and futuristic styling. Citroen were a two-model company for many years until the Ami 6s joined 2CVs, and finally the GS plugged the huge gap. The DS range was diverse, often confusing, and expensive to build. Citroen replaced. it with the

115

THE POST WAR TOURING CAR

equally advanced CS cars in 1974, and have now been merged, reputedly against their will, to the Peugeot combine.

Every company has its blind spot, and in Citroen's case it was over engines. The old DS19 engines were agricultural, and even the latest DS/CX units are rough and lumpy. Only the SM's vee-6 (designed by Maserati) approaches modernity, and the car is extremely expensive.

Citroen in the early '70s used to control Maserati, in Italy.

Daimler   *Cars made in Coventry*   *First Daimler car sold in 1896*

Daimler kept busy during the Second War building buses, trucks, and military vehicles, including the legendary Scout Cars. Their post-war products were almost entirely graceful and gracious touring cars and limousines, ranging up to the ponderous Straight Eight. The Lanchester *marque* name provided an excuse to build smaller cars such as the Leda, and the still-born Sprite.

Under Sir Bernard Docker, Daimler also conceived the successful 2.4-litre Conquest series, which enjoyed a brief period in the sporting spotlight. Other models like the Regency sold in tiny numbers, and the Docker regime was characterised by vast and often vulgar Motor Show 'dream cars.' 104s led to Majestics and Majestic Majors, before BSA were glad to sell out their automotive interests to Jaguar. Their final sporting fling was with the SP250 sports car - a fine vee-8 engine, a 'TR3 copy' chassis and an ugly and warpy glassfibre body.

After takeover by Jaguar their individuality was soon suppressed. The V8-250 saloon was an interesting amalgam of Daimler engine and Jaguar Mk II structure, but after that all Daimlers *were* Jaguars, and none the worse for that.

Facel Vega   *Cars made in France*   *First sold in 1954*

Probably the first of the American-engined mongrels in post-war European terms, the big and impressive Facel Vegas relied exclusively on Chrysler vee-8 power at first. They made few concessions to light weight or low cost, and sold in tiny numbers.

Performance was high but service costs were similar. In an effort to increase production the smaller-engined Facellia made its bow in 1959. The engine was Facel's own 1.6-litre, 4-cylinder, twin-cam, producing 115bhp but little more performance than a TR3A. The price (£2,509 in Britain) was far too high to generate sales, and an attempt to cut this by using a Volve unit in its place also failed.

The last Facel Vega was sold in 1965. It was the only really large-engined French car made since 1945, though perhaps the Monica will take over its mantle in the 1970s.

Ferrari   *Cars made at Maranello Italy*   *First car sold in 1946*

Perhaps the best-documented and least understood of all prestige car manufacturers, Ferrari has an unbeatable reputation. Since the 1940s there have been hundreds of different models, saloons, sports coupes, open sports cars, racing sports cars, single seaters, and specials. Ferrari himself learned his racing craft with the Alfa-Romeo cars of the 1920s and 1930s, taking over Alfa racing activities for a time on behalf of the factory.

His own Grand Prix cars and sports cars have been fully competitive from 1949 to date - no other manufacturer in the world has been so faithful to motor sport in all its forms.

The first true 'production car Ferraris' were based on the 250GT theme - front-engined vee-12 twin-cam or four-cam 3-litre engines, with superb engineering and often surprisingly crude bodywork.

There have been four-seater saloons since the turn of the 1960s, and a succession of fiercer and yet fiercer coupes. Ferrari's first mid-engine road car was the 206 Dino of 1968, and his Daytona of the same period probably the world's fastest production car. Ferrari has relied heavily on Fiat money to finance its racing for some years, and has been controlled by the Turin-based giant since 1969.

Fiat   *Cars made in Turin and other Italian centres*   *First car sold 1899*

Fiat are much the largest of the Italian car makers, and the largest Italian corporation in private hands. Since the Second War their main function has been to supply millions of cars from the tiny 500s to the prestigious 130s, with very few gaps in between.

Their first post-war sports coupe was the exclusive 8V, but it was with the 850, 124 Sport and Dino coupes that their sporting image really blossomed. Many Fiat saloons have been sporting and fun to drive, and Fiat (with Alfa-Romeo) make more twin-cam engines than any other car company.

Fiat finances went from strength to strength in the 1960s, and apart from controlling Autobianchi, they bought control of Ferrari, took over the bankrupt Lancia business, and opened marketing links with Citroen of France.

Since then they have also bought Abarth (who run their racing and rallying team), but have loosened their ties with Citroen.

Fiat began to lose money for the first time in decades, in the early 1970s, and constant labour troubles are hampering their development. Recent models have been much less sporting and more utilitarian than in the past.

Ford (America)   *Cars made in Detroit*   *First sold in 1896*

Henry Ford was the first to embrace true mass-production techniques in car manufacture, and ruled his company with a despotic hand until the Second War. Afterwards Ford preferred to supply millions of 'Detroit-iron' to building sports cars. Their compact and nicely styled Thunderbird came along in 1954, and looked attractive to American sportsmen, but grew up within a few years into a rather horrid 'personal' four-seater.

Ford returned to motor sport, world wide, in 1963, and soon backed this new ambition with the Mustang. Announced in 1964, the Mustang was a spendidly versatile machine which notched hundreds of competition successes. By 1970, however, it had succumbed to the usual Detroit disease of putting on weight with each succeeding model. Safety regulations and exhaust emission restrictions killed off exciting variants like the 'Boss'.

Ford are now in the vanguard of the economy and small car cult in the United States, and eschew performance cars altogether.

THE POST WAR TOURING CAR

Ford (Great Britain)   *Cars made at Dagenham and Halewood*   *First (British) cars sold in 1911*

Since 1945 Ford have achieved a miraculous marketing transformation. At first they were unashamed mass-producers, with no sporting cars at all. They achieved competition successes with the most unpromising cars (Anglias in the 1940s, Zephyrs in the 1950s), but could not change their image. The Detroit decision to emphasise sport revolutionised the British company's fortunes. 1963 saw the arrival of the Cortina GT, and sponsorship of the Lotus-Cortina (see Lotus for details). With the Escort in 1968 came the exciting Twin-cam model, which spawned the Mexico, the RS1600 and finally the RS2000 - all of which have been built at a special 'Advanced Vehicles' factory.

No new Ford range would be complete without its 'GT' variant, and the company's products are infinitely more roadworthy than they were a generation ago.

Ford's involvement in Grand Prix racing (through Keith Duckworth and Cosworth) is now legendary; their own competition activities are serious and successful, with Capris and Escorts. Strangely enough, Ford have never produced their own sports cars though Lotus and other concerns leaned heavily on Ford parts for their own products.

Frazer Nash   *Cars made at Isleworth, Middlesex*   *First sold in 1924*

Frazer Nash sports cars were always made in tiny numbers. At the close of the war, the Adlingtons were instrumental in acquiring BMW designs and engineers to help themselves and Bristols to make post-war machinery. Originally the Bristol was to be a Frazer Nash Bristol, and there were financial links between the two companies, but nothing came of this. Instead, it was agreed that Bristol should make touring cars, and Frazer Nash the sports cars in a very loose association.

No four-seater Frazer Nash was built in the post-war period, but much of the *marque's* successes had an effect on other developments. Sales continued on a tiny scale, and the company's competition successes were legion.

At the end of the 1950s there were attempts to marry the BMW vee-8 engine to a Frazer Nash chassis, but little came of it. In the meantime the Adlingtons were building up their Porsche concession, and no Frazer Nash, not even a prototype, was shown at Earls Court after 1958.

Gordon-Keeble   *Cars made at Southampton*   *First sold in 1964*

The Gordon GT prototype, undoubtedly a sensation when first shown in 1960 at the Geneva Motor show, was the brainchild of John Gordon, whose previous links had been with Peerless and the Peerless GT car. The Gordon was one of the very first cars to combine American horsepower (Chevrolet vee-8) with Italian styling (by Bertone) and a four-seat 2-door saloon body.

Production took time to arrange and finance, and the production cars eventually appeared as Gordon-Keebles (with Jim Keeble as a co-director at this stage). Only about 100 were ever sold, all at almost ludicrously low prices - the 1965 production car, with 5.3-litre vee-8 engine and 135 mph performance sold for an incredible £3,627 when the less habitable Aston Martin DB5 cost £4,412. No-one made money out of the venture, and within a couple of years the *marque* had died. Attempts to revive it failed. The car itself was well-engineered and most roadworthy, as examples which survive confirm.

Gilbern   *Cars made in Llantwit Fardre, South Wales*   *Cars first sold in 1960*

The Gilbern's claim to fame is that it is the only production car ever made in Wales. The original company was founded by Giles Smith and Bernard Frieze and the products always followed the classic formula of tubular chassis, clothed in glassfibre bodywork, with mass produced BMC or Ford mechanical items.

Like many other such companies, finance and profitability was often a problem, and sales were small. 11 cars were built in 1960, with sales rising to 157 in 1965. For some years the staple product was the Gilbern GT, with MGA/MGB engines and BMC suspension and transmission parts - usually bought from the local distributor!

The Genie arrived in 1966, with its Ford vee-6 3-litre engine and new multi-tube chassis. The styling was attractive and Alfa-like though the car was lamentably under-developed when sales began. The Genie became the Invader, and a short-lived Estate version was produced, but financial trouble intervened in 1972 and 1973.

An exciting-looking mid-engined coupe cost too much to develop, and the last Invader was made and sold in 1974.

Healey (and Austin-Healey)   *Cars made in Warwick*   *First car sold in 1946*

It is important not to confuse Healeys with Austin-Healeys. All the Healeys were built by the Healey Motor Company in Warwick, while all but a few Austin-Healeys were assembled in BMC or British Leyland factories.

Donald Healey already had an illustrious reputation when he founded his own car-making company at the close of the War. In the 1930s he had been Technical Director of Triumph for some years. His Healeys were based round a robust but simple chassis frame, with Riley 2½-litre engines and other components. Bodywork was bought out, from small concerns like Westland, Tickford and Abbott.

Between 1946 and 1952 there were many variations on the original theme, with four-seat touring cars (saloons and open cars) and sports 2-seaters all available, but thereafter all were overshadowed by the enormous success of the new Healey 100 2-seater. Apart from the original Riley-engined cars, there were Nash-Healeys and Alvis-Healeys; 1,185 Healey cars were built in this period.

The Healey 100 became the Austin-Healey 100 at the 1952 Motor Show when it was adopted by Austin's Len Lord. The Healey Motor Company actually assembled the first few cars with the help of hand-built bodies from Jensen, after which production was transferred to Longbridge.

Healeys also designed the original Sprite, also adopted by BMC and made at Abingdon, where it threw off an MG Midget variant and is still in production today. The last Austin-Healey Sprite rolled out of Abingdon in 1971.

The Healey Motor Company still exists, but from 1953 to the late 1960s built only short runs of special Austin-Healeys, prototypes, Le Mans cars and the like. The Healey family themselves were brought into Jensen in 1970 and the Jensen-Healey, announced in 1972, was originally Geoff Healey's layout.

The original Healey Motor Company has now been sold off and Donald Healey is now semi-retired.

119

THE POST WAR TOURING CAR

Invicta   *Cars made in Virginia Water, Surrey*   *Cars first sold in 1925*

The fortunes of Invicta and Railton were intermingled in the 1930s and 1940s. Invicta cars disappeared in 1934, and the Railton cars were then assembled in the same factory until the end of the decade.

Bolstered up a little by war-time earnings and post-war enthusiasm, Invicta showed a very advanced prototype, the Black Prince. A company as large as Jaguar might have been able to cope but Invicta, with its tiny capital resources and ill-equipped factories stood little chance. The Black Prince had a sturdy separate cruciform chassis, all independent suspension (torsion bars front and rear), and an exciting-looking twin-ohc 3-litre engine, driving through the Brockhouse Turbo-transmitter 'gearbox'. Full five-seater coachwork on the 10ft. wheelbase could be from several coachbuilders - among whom Jensen and Charlesworth built prototypes.

Only a handful of cars were made, and by 1949 Invicta was finally dead.

Iso   *Cars made in Milan, Italy*   *Cars first sold in 1963*

Rivoltas, Grifos, Leles and other Iso models all stemmed from a design first shown in 1962. The company struggled on, making few cars each year, until the end of 1974, when it finally went into liquidation. Originally financed by Signor Rivolta, and designed by Ing. Bizzarrini, the cars used pressed-steel platform chassis, Bertone or Ghia bodies, and vee-8 Chevrolet engines. Bizzarrini left to make his own cars, the Bizzarrini sports-coupe being very closely related to the 2-seater Grifo coupe.

In recent years a switch was made from Chevrolet to Ford engines, but the energy crisis and rocketing petrol costs hit Iso hard.

Most Isos were four-seaters, the Rivolta being a two-door saloon. Their only four-door saloon was the Fidia, one of the company's final products.

Jaguar   *Cars made in Coventry*   *Cars first sold (as SS) in 1931*

Jaguar entered the 1940s with an excellent reputation, embellished with each succeeding model. William Lyons' original products were sidecars, then special coachwork for other cars. He finally launched the SS car in 1931 - and was the only successful new car maker of the 1930s.

After the war, production re-opened with 1½, 2½, and 3½-litre saloons of pre-war design. Since then Jaguar dates to remember with interest are 1948 (release of the XK120 with its twin-ohc engine, now a living lengend), 1951 (the first Le Mans win, with the XK120C), 1950 (introduction of the Mk 7 - the first 100 mph Jaguar saloon), 1955 (introduction of the integral-construction 2.4-litre saloon), 1961 (the public's first view of the E-Type), 1968 (announcment of the XJ6 series) and 1972 (release of the now-famous vee-12 XJ engine). The company's latest masterpiece is the XJS.

Jensen   *Cars made at West Bromwich, Staffs*   *Cars first sold in 1935*

The Jensen car was incidental to a body-construction business in the beginning, and cars were not the prime product until the 1950s. The first post-war design (appropriately called the PW) had a Meadows engine which was a failure, soon replaced by the ubiquitous 4-litre Austin. PWs led to Interceptors, 541s and CV-8s, before the Interceptors (and FFs) were shown in 1966.

Production volume was low until recent years, by any standards. Even in the early 1970s 30 Interceptors a week was considered high.

Much of Jensen's profit came from contract body-building or final assembly, including A40 Sports for BMC, Austin-Healeys for BMC, Sunbeam Tigers for Rootes, and - not least - Volvo P1800s for the Swedish company.

Jensen almost foundered in the 1960s, was bought and sold several times, and was finally purchased by Kjell Qvale in 1970, who then brought in the Healey family and their designs. The result was the Lotus-engined Jensen-Healey, launched in 1972, which then made up the majority of production. The company finally ceased trading in 1976.

Jensen's four-wheel-drive FF (with bodywork nearly identical to the Interceptor) was the world's only production 4WD machine from 1966 to 1971, but only several hundreds were made.

Jowett　　*Cars made at Idle, Bradford*　　*First cars sold in 1910*

Jowett owes its 'sports saloon' reputation to one model - the Javelin. The Idle-based company had existed for many years by selling rugged but stark little cars with flat-twin and latterly flat-four engines; this apart, there was no question of technical advance.

Gerald Palmer joined Jowett to design the post-war car, announced in 1947 but not properly in production until 1948. In spite of a lengthy gestation period there were serious technical failings in the engines, not solved until the early 1950s. This apart, the Javelin was made in considerable quantity, with coachwork by Briggs Motor Bodies at Doncaster.

To join the Javelin, Jowett also sponsored the Javelin sports car (originally the ERA-Javelin) from an ERA design, which nevertheless needed much development before production began in 1950.

Even more interesting were the special Le Mans Jupiters (with design now controlled by Roy Lunn), and the R4 sports cars which appeared in prototype form.

Jowett were still in desperate mechanical trouble, and it was probably a series of transmission defects which caused collapse. Undelivered bodies piled up at Briggs when production lagged, and by 1954 the car plant had been closed - soon to be sold to International Harvester.

Lagonda　　*Cars made at Staines and Feltham and Newport Pagnell*　　*First cars sold in 1906*

Lagonda fortunes had been revived in the 1930s when W.O. Bentley joined them as Technical Director. His vee-12 engine (built 1936 to 1939) is a classic design.

In post-war years the decision was taken to build an all-new car, with all-independent suspension, and a new Bentley-designed 2.6-litre twin-ohc engine. The sheet steel shortage, and uncertainty about the future, threw Lagonda into David Brown's empire in 1947, whereupon W.O.Bentley left the company.

The Lagonda was produced in saloon and drop-head coupe form, with one very attractive re-style, until the mid-1950s. Its engine was given to the David Brown Aston Martins, being used until 1959.

121

THE POST WAR TOURING CAR

The Lagonda name was revived twice - as the short-lived Rapide saloon (Aston Martin DB4 based) in the early 1960s, and as the Aston Martin Lagonda model (Vee-8 based) in 1974, of which four only were made.

Aston-Martin-Lagonda, sold by the David Brown group a few years earlier, failed financially at the end of 1974. It was again revived in 1975/76 and the Newport Pagnell factory continues to make fine cars.

Lamborghini   *Cars made at S'Agata, Bolognese*   *First cars sold in 1963*

Ferruccio Lamborghini was a Ferrari-owner who thought he could build better cars. He commissioned a splendid new vee-12 engine and conventional chassis and announced his 350GT as an outright Ferrari-competitor.

The new factory, at S'Agata near Modena, now makes a range of spendidly-engineered cars in true high-performance tradition. Lamborghini himself has now relinquished financial control though remaining president of a company that was teetered near to financial breakdown on occasion.

The 4-ohc vee-12 has powered machinery like the Jarama, the 4-seater Espada, and the self-indulgent Miura, not to mention the very fierce mid-engined Countach. There is also the mid-engined Urraco with its vee-8 engine.

Lamborghini's first sensation was the transverse mid-engine Miura, which sold beyond his wildest hopes; this has now been replaced by the even faster 4-litre Countach.

Lamborghinis have never been raced by their sponsors, though the engineering would certainly be worthy of the effort. Theirs is an exclusively high-priced market, and in modern conditions the future must be considered doubtful.

Lanchester   *Cars made in Coventry*   *First car sold in 1900*

Along with Wolseley, Lanchester is one of *the* oldest British car makers. Taken over by Daimler in 1931, by 1945 they were completely integrated into the Daimler group.

Post-war designs were staid and reliable, though the export-only Leda gave rise to Daimler's successful Conquest models. Lanchester had plans for a technically-interesting Sprite model in the mid-1950s, which was to combine a 1.6-litre engine with the new Hobbs automatic transmission. Prototypes were shown in 1954 and 1955, but did not survive the upheaval caused by the sacking of Sir Bernard Docker and other associates.

There has been no Lanchester in production since then, and the company name, via Daimler and Jaguar, is now owned by British Leyland.

Lancia   *Cars made in Turin, Italy*   *First cars sold in 1908*

A family-owned firm until 1969, when their future was assured by a Fiat takeover, Lancia built nothing less than fine cars at any time. Like Alfa-Romeo, they were always overshadowed in production volume by Fiat in Italy, but rarely in engineering or competition pedigree.

In the late 1930s the Aprilia won many fans, while in post-war years the Appias and Aurelias were favourites. Lancia engines were usually in vee-configuration, their Flavia (a flat-four) being the only exception. Lancia raced with great success in the 1950s (D24s winning the Mille Miglia, Targa Florio, and Carrera Panamericana among other races), and designed Grand Prix cars (the D50s) later handed over to Ferrari for his own use.

The Fulvia, particularly the elegant Coupe, was a 1960s success, but expensive to build, and bankruptcy caused the Lancia family to sell out for a nominal million lira (*and all the losses*) in 1969. Fiat retain the name, and have sponsored highly successful new models (the Betas and the mid-engined Stratos).

Lancia still contest races and rallies with great success. Their Stratos (with its vee-6 Ferrari engine) is a world-beater, fast and very strong.

Lea-Francis   *Cars made in Coventry*   *Cars first sold in 1902*

After a period of suspended animation in the 1930s, Lea-Francis returned with a nicely-engineered range late in the decade. After 1945 these cars (with engines closely resembling the contemporary Rileys) carried on with new coachwork for several years. However, there was not enough money available for new models, and the end came in 1953. Saloons and a few rugged but smart sports cars were made with 12hp or 14hp engines; the larger engine was developed to power the early Connaught racing cars.

A half-hearted attempt was made to get back into the car-making business with the ugly 4-seater Lynx roadster. A longer-wheelbase saloon was also planned and we must all be grateful that they never went into production.

Lea-Francis was then taken over by Quinton Hazell, and is now, therefore, owned ultimately by the Burmah Oil conglomerate.

Lotus   *Cars made in Hornsey, Cheshunt and Hethel (Norfolk)*   *First road car (Elite) sold 1959*

Colin Chapman is the post-war equivalent of Sir Williams Lyons. His is the only *marque* to be founded and grow to a respectable size in recent years in this country. Chapman himself had aero-industry technical training, and early Lotuses were all famed for being ultra-light and aerodynamically advanced.

Lotus' first road car was the Elite, built until 1964, but Lotus really joined the big league with the Elan and the Lotus-Cortina, both using the now-famous twin-cam Ford-based engine. Elites never made much money for Lotus, but subsequent models have done so. The Lotus-Cortina was Ford's way of getting into saloon car racing without over-exerting themselves; they were happy for Chapman to build the cars until it became clear that much-improved reliability and better build standards were needed. Ford took over Mk 2 Lotus-Cortina production themselves.

Elans, Elan Plus Twos, and recently the new Elite all used the backbone chassis principle. The mid-engined Europa (originally Renault-engined in 1966 and for export only) followed the same technical path.

No one has to be reminded of Lotus' racing record, or of their technical bravery. Prices have soared in recent years, and the Elites and related models are right out of the average enthusiast's reach. Lotus now make their own engines and much of their transmissions - the engines were also supplied to Jensen for the Jensen-Healey model.

THE POST WAR TOURING CAR

Marauder   *Cars made in Dorridge, Warwicks*   *First car sold in 1950*

Marauder sports tourers were the creation of three Rover engineers - Wilks, King and Mackie. The chassis was almost entirely Rover 75, as were mechanical details, and even the coachwork had recognisable Rover touches.

Very few - a mere 15 examples - were built, and as Spen King remembers: "The cost of making them rose faster than the price we felt we could charge for them." Production closed down after a very short run, though the model name trade mark was subsequently sold to General Motors in Detroit.

Mercedes-Benz   *Cars made in Stuttgart, West Germany*   *First Benz car was made in 1885*

There is little doubt that Papa Benz made the world's first practicable car. Benz combined with Daimler, then gave birth to the Mercedes in the early 1900s.

In 1945 Mercedes were bombed out due to Allied action. Production got going again with pre-war Type 180s. Once the Mercedes design-machine began to churn they soon regained their reputation. The big 300 and 220 saloons were soon followed by the 300SL and 190SL sports cars (in 1954). Earlier the 300SL had won at Le Mans in 1952 - the production car had the still unique space-frame chassis, and fuel-injection, plus the famed gull-wing coupe body style.

In the last 20 years there has been a succession of solid, ultra-safe, carefully-engineered saloons, ranging up to the latest 'S class' cars, and not forgetting the titanic and complex 600 saloons and limousines.

Mercedes swept the motor racing board in 1954 and 1955 with the W196 and 300SLR designs, then retired, never to appear again. As a publicity exercise, a handful of mid-engined multi-rotor Wankel C111 coupes were made in 1969, but nothing came of these.

The modern Mercedes range is wide and complex, with an important number of diesel-powered versions. Their safety standards and quality requirements are probably unsurpassed in modern times.

MG   *Cars made at Abingdon, Berkshire*   *First car sold in 1924*

'By Cecil Kimber, out of Morris Garages' is one way to define the origin of the MG cars. Originally special Morris-based sports cars, their appeal was widened in the late 1930s.

The early post-war MG Y saloons, an amalgam of Morris Eight and Ten components, were pleasant and precise performers, but did not long survive the formation of BMC. The ZA and ZB Magnettes, with tuned BMC 'B' Series engines, were better cars than many will admit, though their Austin-Morris successors, Farina-styled, were dreadful. Even the MG1100s and 1300s, tuned and tarted-up variations of the Morris 1100 theme, were devoid of character, and MG's name only lives on in sports cars. The MGB dates from 1962, and the Midget basically from 1958. Both are much overdue for replacement, and their future in British Leyland must be in doubt.

Peerless   *Cars made in Slough*   *First car sold in 1958*

A typical combination of square-section multi-tubular frame, glassfibre bodyshell and large manufacturer (Triumph, on this occasion) mechanicals, the Peerless was a vain attempt to build a profitable, low-production, 4-seater saloon. Conceived by John Gordon and Jim Keeble (see Gordon-Keeble), the car used Triumph TR3 engine, transmission, axle and suspension items, and had a limited following.

After the usual financial crises, Peerless production creased in 1959 and after a period the car was re-born as the Warwick. This *marque* fared little better, even though a Buick-engined version was proposed, and the last car was built in 1962. The original sponsors, by then, were involved in the Gordon-Keeble project; Warwicks were made by Bernie Rodger Developments at Colnbrook.

Porsche   *Cars made in Stuttgart, West Germany*   *First car sold in 1948*

Dr. Porsche already a famous name, even before the car bearing it was released. Between the wars he had been responsible, among other cars for the Austro-Daimlers, for the SSK and SSKL Mercedes-Benz machines, for the mid-engine vee-16 Auto-Union GP car of 1934, and - most important of all - for the design of the KdF-Wagen, the 'People's car', the now legendary Volkswagen 'Beetle'.

The first Porsches were very much VW-specials, but evolved gradually and firmly over the years until all traces of VW ancestry had disappeared. The original flat-four, rear-engined coupe design continued in recognisable, though much-modified, form until the mid-1960s, with the Carrera Two as the fastest and most effective of all.

From 1964 Porsche sales have centred around the very desirable 911 series, whose variants have become ever faster, more roadworthy and expensive.

Racing Porsches have been winners for a generation, and none are more famous than the fabulous 917s, with their flat-12 engines in normally-aspirated or turbocharged guise.

Porsche have a renowned consultant engineering laboratory, and their patented work is licensed to other car makers all over the world.

Reliant   *Cars made at Tamworth, Staffs*   *First 4-wheeler car sold in 1962*

The Sabre sports car arrived in 1961, but before then Reliant had been making three-wheelers powered by the old Austin Seven engine since the 1930s. Three-wheelers continue to be very important to Reliant's commercial survival, and have had their own engines since 1964.

Sabres were mainly made from 'bought-out' components, and were rather horrid. These crude Ford-engined sports cars were displaced by the much-improved Scimitars in 1964, and the GTE followed in 1968. The company's products have steadily moved 'up market', as a glance at the latest sports-coupe-estate GTE confirms. All Scimitars have had separate chassis, glassfibre bodies of unusually high quality, and Ford power trains.

All Reliant four-wheelers except the unsuccessful Rebel have been aimed at the sporting market. Production is, however, overshadowed by the mass of Robins and vans which flow from the three-wheeler production lines.

Like Lotus, Reliant are not linked to a large car concern, though they are themselves controlled by a large finance house.

THE POST WAR TOURING CAR

Renault   *Cars made in Paris and other French locations*   *First car sold in 1898*

The second war was cruel to Renault. Bombing destroyed the factories, and Renault himself was imprisoned, accused of collaboration with the enemy. The company was at once nationalised, and is now an outstandingly successful example of such an enterprise.

Post-war production started with the oddly-styled 4cv, but built up rapidly when the Dauphine took over. Renault themselves have not yet made sports cars, though the R16s, 15s and 17s all have performance capabilities. Renault is now the largest of all French car makers.

Their 'rear engine' philosophy was reversed at the beginning of the 1960s - all Renault cars now having front-wheel drive layouts.

French sporting-car concerns like Alpine relied heavily on Renault for mechanical parts, and Alpine-Renault soon became famous in racing and rallying. Gordini also had links with the Regie, and with Alpine; Alpine-Renault are now owned by Renault, continue to build rear-engined coupes at Dieppe, and run the entire racing and competition programme, which has embraced Le Mans, Formula Two and the Formule Renault in recent years.

Riley   *Cars made in Coventry, Abingdon and Cowley*   *First car sold in 1898*

By 1945 the independent Riley company had disappeared. This had foundered financially in 1938 and been swallowed by Nuffield. Post-war Rileys were built by MG, and were individually-styled, with the familiar Riley twin-camshaft engines under the bonnets.

Rising costs and falling demand caused BMC to introduce 'rationalised' Rileys in the 1950s, primarily with the old engine but eventually with BMC pushrod ohv designs. The last real Rileys were the 1½ and 2½-litre saloons, the last even with a Riley engine was the Pathfinder. After that only the name was original, as all were tarted up Wolseleys (which themselves were no longer true Wolseleys!).

The Mini-based 'Elf' was a disgraceful use of a once-famous name, as was the 1100-based Kestrel. The last of these shameful machines was sold in 1969.

Rootes   *Cars made in Coventry and Linwood*   *First 'Rootes' car sold in 1932*

In the 1930s Rootes absorbed Hillman, Humber, Sunbeam and Talbot - but by 1945 no trace remained. Post-war cars, whatever their badges, were 'Rootes' designs.

Post-war prosperity was always based on big sellers like the Hillman Minx and the Humber Hawk. The only sports car to come from the factory was the Sunbeam Alpine (of two varieties, on early 1950s Sunbeam-Talbot chassis, and on late 1950s Minx/Husky chassis parts).

Sporting cars were called Sunbeam-Talbots and later Sunbeams, achieving some sporting reputation because of a steadfast competition programme masterminded by Norman Garrad.

Original Sunbeams died off in 1955 as sales dropped, and later Rapiers were hot Minxes which improved over the years.

The Imp was the car which broke Rootes, though a 3-month strike at a London body-making factory hastened the end. Chrysler bought control in 1968, and have been removing all traces of individuality ever since.

A few hot Imps and a few hot Avengers remain to give flavour to a very dull organisation. There are close links with Simca in France, also owned by Chrysler.

Rover   *Cars made in Solihull*   *First car sold in 1904*

Independent in 1945, Rover bought Alvis in 1965, were themselves taken over by Leyland-Triumph in 1967, and have now disappeared into the British Leyland organisation, commercially and operationally merged with Triumph.

The Wilks influence saved Rover from bankruptcy in the 1930s, and built up an impressive 'quality' image. Post-war cars were universally dull - like the famous old P4s and P5s - but the string of gas-turbine-powered prototypes (designed by Spen King), and the profit-earning Land Rover showed that the engineering know-how was present.

With a limited rallying programme in the 1960s, and a link with BRM to build a gas-turbine racing sports car to change the image, Rover then unveiled the Rover 2000 cars in 1963.

A vee-8 engine design bought from General Motors heralded great things; the promise was stifled when Leyland cancelled Spen King's exciting mid-engined P6BS coupe, and cancelled the P8 saloon project, but 1976 sees the first of a new generation of up-to-date Rovers.

Saab   *Cars built at Trollhattan, Sweden*   *First car sold in 1950*

Designed by a company whose speciality was originally aeroplanes, the first Saab showed all signs of such parentage. There were no pre-war Saabs, and each and every one has been given front-wheel drive. 92s, 93s and 96s all looked much the same, all very strong, and all with an impressively rugged competition record.

The 96 was one of the very last two-stroke powered cars ever built (Wartburg will probably be the last), and to replace it Saab bought first from Ford Germany, then from Triumph in Coventry.

There have been occasional flirtations with coupes such as the Sonnett, but Saabs are not noted for flashing performance. Saloons driven by such as Erik Carlsson and Stig Blomqvist have proved that performance isn't everything.

Saab, still making superbly modern fighter planes, have now merged with Scania-Vabis, whose lorries are the 'Rolls-Royce' of the commercial vehicle business.

Singer   *Cars finally made in Coventry*   *First car sold in 1905*

In the 1930s Singer made cars in considerable volume, with models like the Bantam and the Le Mans Sports car figuring strongly. In the 1940s and 1950s, the company struggled with old engines and out-dated styling. Engines were used by HRG, and a single-ohc 1500 had promise, but the financial end came in 1955 when Rootes made a bid for the company.

Singer was another Rootes *marque* until 1970, when the name finally disappeared. The last Singers were either modified Hunters or modified Imps, with no individuality of their own.

THE POST WAR TOURING CAR

Studebaker   *Cars made in America, latter at South Bend*   *First car sold in 1902*

One of America's smallest car makers, Studebaker shot to prominence in the 1950s with Loewy-styling on the coupes, and finally with the Avanti coupe. There were no out-and-out sporting cars; indeed Studebaker's survival depended on the sale of cheap 'compact cars' in their last few years.

Mergers and rationalisation could only delay the end, which came in 1966. More recently, production of the striking Avanti was resumed by a tiny concern, using General Motor engines. Its disappearance is now only a matter of time, and no replacement is expected.

Triumph   *Cars made in Coventry and Liverpool*   *First car sold in 1923*

In 1939 the original Triumph company was broke. During the war the remains were bought by Standard, and in 1946 production of Standard-designed Triumphs began.

Activities have since been completely integrated with Standard; indeed it was Standard's name which was axed in 1963 while Triumph prospered. The long-lived TR series is now legendary, though the Heralds, Spitfires and 2000/2.5 PI series have all pleased sporting drivers.

From the late 1950s, Michelotti styling established a recognisable house line, only now being dispersed. Commercially Standard-Triumph have had a chequered time. They were taken over by Leyland in 1961, merged with Rover in 1967, and became part of British Leyland in 1968. The Rover-Triumph operation is now completely integrated and future model policy decided by common executives.

Triumph cars claim many quantity-production firsts in Britain including all-independent sports cars, front wheel disc brakes, and fuel-injection.

Vauxhall   *Cars made at Luton and Ellesmere Port*   *First car sold in 1903*

The 30/98 was a famous 'vintage' competitor for Bentleys, and Pomeroy-designed cars raced on many occasions; takeover by General Motors followed in 1926. Thereafter, production expanded quickly and all traces of 'character' were lost.

Post-war products have generally been dull, even horrid - as the first Victors show. There were half-hearted attempts in the 1960s to inject performance into the range with VX4/90s and Brabham-Vivas.

Engineering has improved dramatically in recent years, and a credible racing/rallying programme by DTV has transformed the sportsman's view of the models. The overhead-cam slant-four engine formed the original basis of the Lotus/Jensen twin-cam; many parts are interchangeable.

Vauxhall's first outright sporting coupe - the droop-snoot Firenza - appeared in 1973, but few seem to have been made.

Volvo   *Cars made at Gothenburg, Sweden*   *First car sold in 1927*

Almost all Volvos are solid, reliable, long-lasting saloons and estates. Since 1945 there have only been four basic models, each with its own sporting version in the line-up. Strength and balance count for much in rallying, where Volvos often excelled; lately they have been left behind in the power race.

Only one attempt at a sporting car was made - with the P1800, originally with Pressed Steel bodyshell and Jensen final assembly. Production soon returned to Sweden, and in the end there was a final attempt to match the Scimitar GTE with the 1800E.

In recent years Volvo have embraced vehicle safety, and their latest models are excellent examples of safety engineering coming before styling or performance.